"Amy Saltzman takes the mystery out of mindfulness by introducing easily understood concepts and practical activities that can be immediately applied to any sport. This is a valuable resource for athletes of all levels, as well as coaches who want to help their athletes and teams perform mindfully."

—**Pete Kirchmer**, mPEAK (mindfulness Performance Enhancement Awareness and Knowledge); director of the University of California, San Diego's Center for Mindfulness; mindfulness-based health coach

"In every athletic career, there are crucial moments—moments when an athlete's inner voice can make or break her performance. Being mindful and present in these moments is the key to athletic success. And yet athletes, coaches, and parents often overlook *how* to do just that. This book will become your new guide and will ensure, when *your* moments come, that you will be ready."

—**John O'Sullivan**, founder of the Changing the Game Project, and author of *Changing the Game*

"In my experience, the path to being your best, in sports and in life, always passes through the Still Quiet Place. Learning how to get there will prepare you for any challenge you might face. If you are ready to put in the same degree of work mentally as you do physically, the steps outlined in this book will help you get to the next level of your game."

—**Cassidy Lichtman**, two-time first-team All-American at Stanford University in volleyball; gold medalist in the Pan American Games, 2015; silver medalist in the Grand Champions Cup, 2013; assistant coach for the 2016 NCAA Champions at Stanford

"Amy Saltzman's *A Still Quiet Place for Athletes* is a superb introduction to mindfulness and its practical application for athletes and coaches. This compelling, accessible book will help you achieve elite-level performance success!"

—**Cornelia Cannon Holden, MDiv**, team building, leadership development, and sports psychology coach for US Women's Ice Hockey (2006-2010); CEO at Mindful Warrior (www.mindfulwarrior.com)

"In *A Still Quiet Place for Athletes*, Amy Saltzman gives real strategies and techniques that are not just for athletes, but for coaches, teachers, and parents who see athletics as preparation for life. All I can say is I wish I had this book as a kid growing up in my sports-obsessed childhood."

—**Tim Ryan**, US representative from Ohio and author of *A Mindful Nation*

"*A Still Quiet Place for Athletes* is an instructive and interactive tool, tailor-made for athle level of competition. The book offers a wide range of skills related to achieving peak perfc including mindfulness, self-care, how to face challenges, and creating habits of exce Overall, this book is a great instrument for practitioners and coaches who work with athlete pursue excellence in their sport."

—**Logan Lyons**, PhD candidate and sport psychology consultant

"Mindfulness is a practice to pay attention to the here and now. Every athlete and coach knows the value of that. This book helps you get there more habitually."

—**Dan Quinn**, head coach of the Atlanta Falcons of the National Football League (NFL)

"I am energized after reading Amy Saltzman's *A Still Quiet Place for Athletes*. This unique text fills an important gap in our field, and has the potential to be a wonderful resource for athletes, coaches, and practitioners. The book affords the reader not just the *what*, but also the *how* when it comes to achieving peak performance. Specifically, it highlights strategies for readers to seek their own inner 'quiet' through mindfulness, self-care, and the creation of habits of excellence."

—**Travis Dorsch, PhD**, assistant professor of human development and family studies, and founding director of the Utah State University Families in Sport Lab

"*A Still Quiet Place for Athletes* is an amazing, comprehensive book that covers all the bases and addresses the concerns of athletes, coaches, and parents, for both sports and life. Grounded in research, personal experience, and a lifelong commitment to training and developing athletes of all competitive levels to peak performance and access to 'a still quiet place.'"

—**George T. Mumford**, author of *The Mindful Athlete*

"Saltzman has written a practical guide for training mindfulness in sport. She provides concrete tools and real-world applications that are easily accessible for competitive athletes at all levels. *A Still Quiet Place for Athletes* is an outstanding new resource for mental training!"

—**Kelli Moran-Miller, PhD**, licensed psychologist and certified mental performance consultant

"This book offers a step-by-step guide to the skills necessary in achieving peak performance while opening your eyes to the realization that you are so much more than your performance. As a former baseball player, I can see how the lessons taught here are so critical to success in my sport. These are the skills required to consistently slow down a 95-mph fastball, to work through slumps and injuries, and ultimately, to reconnect to one's true essence. Amy Saltzman has provided an essential guide for anyone wanting to find flow in sports and in life."

—**Shawn Green**, two-time Major League Baseball (MLB) All-Star, and author of *The Way of Baseball*

"An astute and comprehensive manual for mindfulness training, *A Still Quiet Place for Athletes* teaches everything needed to achieve 'flow' and peak performance. With a kind and curious voice, Saltzman brings together high intellect; clear, step-by-step instruction; and a warm approach that offers invaluable benefits to athletes in all sports. When a person gets deeply in tune with their thoughts, emotions, and bodily experiences, they can choose the path of awareness and success— this book teaches exactly that."

—**Lisa Mitzel**, NCAA National Champion gymnast; international speaker, clinician, mental training expert, and author of *Focused and On Fire*

MINDFULNESS SKILLS
for *ACHIEVING*
PEAK PERFORMANCE
& FINDING FLOW
in SPORTS & LIFE

A STILL QUIET QUIET PLACE FOR ATHLETES

AMY SALTZMAN, MD

New Harbinger Publications, Inc.

Publisher's Note

This publication is designed to provide accurate and authoritative information in regard to the subject matter covered. It is sold with the understanding that the publisher is not engaged in rendering psychological, financial, legal, or other professional services. If expert assistance or counseling is needed, the services of a competent professional should be sought.

Distributed in Canada by Raincoast Books

Copyright © 2018 by Amy Saltzman
       New Harbinger Publications, Inc.
       5674 Shattuck Avenue
       Oakland, CA 94609
       www.newharbinger.com

Material in chapters 3, 5, 9, and 14 has been adapted from "Mindfulness in Sports" by Amy Saltzman, in TEACHING MINDFULNESS SKILLS TO KIDS AND TEENS, ed. Christopher Willard and Amy Saltzman, copyright © 2015 by Christopher Willard and Amy Saltzman. Used by permission of Guilford Press.

"Autobiography in Five Chapters" by Portia Nelson reprinted with the permission of Beyond Words/ Atria Books, a division of Simon & Schuster, Inc., from THERE'S A HOLE IN MY SIDEWALK: THE ROMANCE OF SELF-DISCOVERY by Portia Nelson. Copyright © 1993 by Portia Nelson. All rights reserved.

Cover design by Amy Shoup

Acquired by Tesilya Hanauer

Edited by James Lainsbury

Library of Congress Cataloging-in-Publication Data on file

20   19   18

10 9 8 7 6 5 4 3 2 1   First Printing

With infinite gratitude for

The Team

Georgina Lindsey, by all accounts a masterful, transformational, and evolutionary coach, and my coach and mentor, thus far, for twenty-nine awe-inspired years;

Eric, my unwaveringly loving husband;

Jason and Nicole, our amazing children;

the brave and true athletes choosing to pursue excellence in sports and life;

and, ultimately, the Still Quiet Place.

Contents

Foreword

Mindfulness and sports are a winning combination, one we have been moving toward since Timothy Gallwey wrote *The Inner Game of Tennis* in 1974. Phil Jackson pioneered mindfulness in professional sports, and we now see some of the highest performers at all levels embracing mindfulness practice. Under Steve Kerr's leadership, the Golden State Warriors made mindfulness one of the team's key values (along with joy, compassion, and competition). And both 2016 World Series teams benefitted from the wisdom of sport psychologists—Ken Ravizza for the Cubs and Charlie Maher for the Indians—who helped players keep their minds in the moment. And this is just to name a few.

Bringing mindfulness to all athletes is a logical next step, so I am excited about Amy Saltzman's *A Still Quiet Place for Athletes*. Having practiced mindfulness myself for many years, I was delighted to be asked by Amy to write this foreword. I was given a month to complete it, so I predictably put it at the back of my to-do list and forgot about it—until the day it was due!

At the time, I was feeling overwhelmed with what seemed like an infinite list of challenges in my work with Positive Coaching Alliance (PCA); the recent passing of my father-in-law Ralph, whom I loved deeply; and the daily issues of being a husband, father, and grandfather. I reminded myself that I had faced challenges that felt overwhelming before, and that my mindfulness practice usually helped me find a way to get them done. But I still remained anxious about upcoming challenges, and regretful about things I had not done well in the past. I felt stuck in what Amy describes as *my feelings having me* rather than *me learning to have my feelings*.

At this point, part of me deeply regretted having agreed to write this foreword in the first place; but, nonetheless, I dove in to her manuscript in search of motivation. Almost immediately I found the phrase, "Noticing what you are experiencing with kindness and curiosity *is* mindfulness." At a mindfulness retreat years ago, I heard a speaker say something similar, that "gentleness with your self is the gateway to courage." While I had embraced that notion at the time, Amy helped me realize that I was now very far away from the kindness toward myself that I encourage athletes to adopt for themselves daily.

As my experience attests, this book offers a place of kindness and curiosity where athletes can simply be in the moment with their thoughts and feelings. It shows that you can choose how you want to respond to any given situation—from writing a foreword to your colleague's book to taking a potentially game-winning shot—rather than react automatically out of anxiety or fear. When I started the PCA nearly twenty years ago, my goal was to help athletes find the pure joy in playing sports that seems all too rare today, and I am grateful to Amy's book for helping me rediscover this same sense of joy when it comes to my own work with mindful athletes.

I am reminded of Fred Rogers, who once said "Life is deep and simple, and what our society gives us is shallow and complicated." This deep simplicity of life is accentuated in sports, which has been called "life with the volume turned up." A *Still Quiet Place for Athletes* can help athletes and coaches find the deep and simple heart of sports. It is filled with insights, exercises, tools, and resources that can help athletes of all ages bring their full self to their sport and to their lives.

A *Still Quiet Place for Athletes* is an important and valuable resource for athletes, coaches, and parents; really, everyone can benefit from its wisdom. Thank you, Amy Saltzman, for providing us with this gift.

*   *   *

Jim Thompson is founder and CEO of Positive Coaching Alliance (http://www.positivecoach .org), a national nonprofit with the goal to use sports to develop "Better Athletes, Better People," and a longtime practitioner of mindfulness meditation.

Introduction

Standing at the chalk box, she dips her hands in the cool smooth fluff, forms it into cakes and lets them sift through her construction worker's calloused hands. The metal and wood structure of the uneven bars taunts her with images of ghost gymnasts accomplishing her goals.

The bars giggle as she mounts, clanking and rattling with her motion. She pushes her body away from the upper bar, and directs it in a pendulum's arc toward the lower bar. At the instant of contact her oyster body snaps shut, its treasure inside. With her nose to her knees, and the bar imbedded in her hinged hips, she circles and snaps open again, stretching to crucify herself on the upper bar. Thud. Her landing mocks her efforts. Again and again she mounts. Each time her pendulum body swings and falls in a dull tick-tock monotony.

The wine-colored bruises on her hips ache and throb, yet she chalks her blistered hands again. Echoes in her mind of an old coach's wise words about plateaus soothe her frustrations.

Once more she swings and falls. Perhaps tomorrow the chalk clouds she claps from her hands will have a silver lining.

The passage was written in 1981 when I was a junior in high school, *looong* before mindfulness came into my life. Yet, unbeknownst to me, gymnastics was my first mindfulness practice. The above passage depicts an athlete's (my) moment-to-moment awareness of physical sensations, thoughts, and feelings. And, my joyful determined spirit!

In the decades since, I have discovered that there is *one essential element* for achieving peak performance—finding, or being found by, your true coach. It is my experience that this coach will have tremendous expertise in training your body, your mind, and your spirit equally. To those of you who feel you have not yet found that person, don't give up—never give up! The very purpose of this book is to train you in the primary distinctions for finding flow.

Body

Like most young athletes, I began my journey at the local rinky-dink gymnastics facility just a few miles from home. (A huge shout-out to rinky-dink sports facilities where so many of us get our start!) "By chance" my mother had a dear friend Kathleen, who, *by chance*, was the head gymnastics coach at the University of Denver. Kathleen in turn pointed me to Max, the director of the youth program who, by chance, was my first *true* coach. I have been extraordinarily lucky and privileged to have found two true coaches in one lifetime.

Like most great coaches, Max progressively developed my physical skills. Exceptionally, he also shared his deep love of anatomy and physiology with every gymnast in his program, whether they were interested or not. He required all beginners to be able to point to and name the major bones, intermediates to be able to point to and name the major muscles, and advanced gymnasts to know the names *and* functions of the all the physiological systems. These remarkable requirements awakened in me a deep respect for and love of the human body and its amazing capacities. Most importantly, Max's heartfelt enthusiasm ensured that in the midst of the daily blunders, falls, stumbles, popped blisters, taping, and all that training and competing entails, there was great joy and flow.

Even with Max's comprehensive strength-and-conditioning regimen, I experienced repeated shoulder dislocations and, ultimately, chose to have reconstructive surgery on my right shoulder at age fourteen and my left shoulder at age fifteen in order to continue to compete. This is sport. Of the many sacrifices and frustrations a competitive athlete accepts, nothing compared to the disappointment of Max relocating to start his own program and family. Despite his departure, I continued to compete through high school. I arrived at college as an unknown, unrecruited, nonscholarship athlete. I showed up, tried out, and earned a spot as a walk-on on the Stanford varsity team. The beginning of my junior year brought a series of injuries, and I chose to stop competing in gymnastics. I briefly became a triathlete, and subsequently a competitive cyclist.

"By chance" one rainy afternoon outside the Stanford post office, where the cycling team usually gathered, I met the man who would become my husband. A much more experienced competitive cyclist, he had wisely ridden earlier in the day and had just come by to see who was going out to ride in the rain (only me). To this day, he continues to compete at the highest levels of the sport.

Spirit

In the summer of 1989, recently married and still cycling, I was eager to start my second year of medical school. "By chance" a cycling friend invited me to attend a retreat with her longtime transformational sports coach, Ms. Georgina Lindsey. (From here on out Ms. Lindsey will be referred to as Coach G.) Thus began the miraculous, all-encompassing, awe-inspiring, soul-based journey that led me to unequivocally *experience* the synergy of body, mind, and spirit—True Flow.

Coach G was, and continues to be, an actual pioneer in the transformational coaching field. She had established her own highly regarded athletics coaching company, Quantum Leap, in Venice, California. In 1986, Transformational Technologies, one of the top corporate coaching franchises, then recruited her to cocreate a division to bring transformation to sports and athletics. At twenty-six she was by far the youngest—and only female—founding partner of Sports Vision. The other founding partners were Rolland Todd, previously the head coach of the Portland Trail Blazers, and William Kasoff, previously the head of the US Tennis Association. Sports Vision was the first national company to bring Transformational Technologies to athletes. While at Sports Vision, Coach G trained athletes in the Women's Sports Foundation; in the LPGA; on the Phoenix Suns; and on a majority of the teams at the University of Nevada, Las Vegas; among others. At the time, Sports Vision's techniques were so profoundly innovative and transformational that other superstars in this emerging field, such as Tim Gallwey, author of *The Inner Game of Tennis*, sought out the expertise of the company's founders and requested to "play" and, periodically, guest coach with them.

In 1989, after the devastating, unfortunate death of the founding partner of the corporate franchise, the founders of Sports Vision went their separate ways. Coach G resumed private coaching and began offering a series of highly regarded workshops for extremely accomplished female athletes. Participants included Suzy Chaffee (downhill-skiing Olympian in 1968 and freestyle world champion in 1971, 1972, and 1973) and Nancy Hogshead (three-time Olympic gold medalist in swimming in 1984).

During my first daylong retreat I sat in a circle with ten other athletes. I don't remember the exercises, the handouts, or the room. I do know that Coach G diagnosed, with masterful precision, each person's "act," the unconscious patterns that prevented her from achieving her truest dreams. My ego (or personality) didn't hear my diagnosis—"poor me"—as good news. However, my spirit was enlivened and elated by the truth.

Over the past three decades Coach G has ardently refined and expanded her offerings and served the gamut of humanity. She supports clients as they deconstruct their "normal" modes of thinking about themselves, their unconscious limitations, and their unrealized possibilities. Her work is exciting, exacting, and provocative. She is the first to acknowledge that her intensity is definitely not for everyone. And those who commit to the rigors of her work *repeatedly* experience astonishing, exhilarating breakthroughs. Bottom line, Coach G is flow.

Oddly enough, or perhaps not, she is also one of the most humble, private individuals I know. She has never had a web page or business cards, and her phone number is unlisted. Go figure. For more than thirty years the many people who have found their way to her have done so by word of mouth. Given her tragic and traumatic childhood, who she is, is all the more astounding. Soon, those fascinated by her will be able to read her courageous, against-all-odds tale in her forthcoming creative-nonfiction memoir, *Naked Grace*.

Mind

"By chance," in the winter of 1990 I had two cycling "accidents" in short succession. Georgina's coaching enabled me to discover that, truly, nothing is *by chance*, and that accidents are always opportunities in disguise. While rehabilitating my knee, I was able to attend to some neglected aspects of my life, including finally joining the American Holistic Medical Association (AHMA). Although I felt pulled to participate in this new world of true health care, I had missed every deadline for the AHMA's annual conference—registration, scholarships, and housing. Utilizing Coach G's distinction of "living from vision versus circumstances," I looked beyond the circumstances and sent in my application. "By chance" another woman canceled at the last minute and I received her registration, scholarship, and housing! After returning from the conference, and receiving coaching, I boldly sent a letter to the AHMA board of trustees suggesting creative ways the organization could nurture the natural holism in medical students and residents. "By chance" four months after that conference I was asked to join the board of the AHMA, and I served as trustee for ten years.

In early 1993, the airing of Bill Moyers's PBS special *Healing and the Mind* was a pivotal event for the holistic medicine community, and for me personally. After seeing the segment on the Stress Reduction Clinic (now called the Center for Mindfulness in Medicine, Health Care, and Society) at the University of Massachusetts, I felt an undeniable urge to practice and share mindfulness. I read the book *Full Catastrophe Living* (1990), written by the clinic's director, Jon Kabat-Zinn, and immediately began a daily mindfulness practice.

Despite having minimal experience with formal practice, an increasingly familiar mixture of arrogance, faith, persistence, and strong intuition compelled me to contact Dr. Kabat-Zinn at the Stress Reduction Clinic—*repeatedly*. Using another of Coach G's distinctions— "outrageous request"—I respectfully asked to participate in comprehensive training in mindfulness-based stress reduction. "By chance" my medical residency director approved my request to devote a month to studying mindfulness. Surprisingly, she also gave me academic credit for attending the program and found funding to pay my tuition! In 1993, I spent the glorious, colorful month of October in western Massachusetts immersed in the practice and study of mindfulness.

When I returned, I designed a large-scale clinical trial to evaluate the benefits of mindfulness for medical patients suffering from chronic pain and illness. Then, after my children were born, I began sharing mindfulness with parents. Over time I simplified and distilled the practices so I could share them with young children and adolescents. Now it is my great joy to share them with you.

Body, Mind, and Spirit

In 1990, upon entering my third year of medical school, I transitioned from being a competitive athlete to being a devoted recreational athlete, running, cycling, and developing a yoga practice. And in 2003, at the age of forty, I began mindfully learning how to snowboard.

For the past twenty-nine years, it has been my great fortune to train with Coach G on a *weekly* basis. In a culture where people go from one self-help workshop to another searching for quick fixes, an ongoing, intimate relationship with a true master (one who has attained mastery) is absolutely priceless. Professionally, her coaching guided me through the transition from competitive athletics, the extremely rigorous and deeply gratifying moments of medical school and residency, and the perils and delights of bringing holism to conventional medicine and mindfulness to local, national, and international K-12 education. More intimately, her coaching has seen me through the highs and lows of marriage, the sweet joys and heartaches of parenting one athlete and one artist, and all of the ordinary and extraordinary experiences that have led to the creation and development of the Still Quiet Place offerings, including this book. Thankfully today, as always, her astonishing combination of keen intuition, fierce clarity, and loving compassion continues to support me in joyfully expressing my deepest passions and creative gifts. This book would not exist without her devoted, unwavering guidance.

It is an absolute privilege to share the practices of mindfulness with you, and to pay Coach G's truly awesome coaching forward—to inspire *you* to find flow in sports and in life.

PART 1

The Fundamentals—Mindfulness

Hello, and congratulations! By choosing to read this book, you are demonstrating that you are an athlete who is committed to training not only your body, but also your mind and spirit. Over time this commitment will allow you to experience flow in sports and in life.

As your first mindfulness exercise, simply notice the thoughts and feelings that appear as you reread this sentence: "By choosing to read this book, you are demonstrating that you are an athlete who is committed to training not only your body, but also your mind and spirit." Maybe you feel a sense of excitement, like *Yes. I'm stoked. I've been looking for something to help me get to the next level.* Maybe you feel doubt and resistance, like *There's no way that just reading a book can help me with my paralyzing precompetition anxiety.* Take a moment and just be really honest with yourself about what you're thinking and feeling…

Excellent! You've just done your first mindfulness practice!

CHAPTER 1

Welcome

Neither mastery nor satisfaction can be found in the playing of any game without giving some attention to the relatively neglected skills of the inner game. This is the game that takes place in the mind of the player, and it is played against such obstacles as lapses in concentration, nervousness, self-doubt and self-condemnation. In short, it is played to overcome all habits of mind which inhibit excellence in performance.

—Tim Gallwey

This chapter provides straightforward, usable definitions and relatable examples of mindfulness and flow. It includes a summary of the research demonstrating the benefits of mindfulness, including how practicing mindfulness can increase the likelihood that you will experience flow. The chapter closes with suggestions for how you can best use this book to achieve peak performance and find flow in sports and in life.

Mindfulness

About now you may be wondering what "mindfulness" is. So, let's begin with a definition:

Mindfulness is paying attention here and now,
with kindness and curiosity,
so that we can choose our behavior.

Let's break this definition down. "Paying attention here and now" means doing our best to not dwell on the past, or worry or fantasize about the future, and simply paying attention to what's actually happening in *this* moment. And we pay attention "with kindness and curiosity." Otherwise we are often incredibly hard on ourselves. We tend to see only where we've "made a mistake" or "screwed up." Rather than judging and critiquing ourselves, with mindfulness we practice bringing an attitude of kindness and curiosity to ourselves and our experience. Finally, when we bring our kind and curious attention to our thoughts and feelings, to the sensations in our bodies, and to the people and circumstances in our lives, then we have all the information we need "so that we can choose our behavior"—that is, respond in the moment to events during training, competition, and daily life.

As you begin, it may encourage you to know that more and more elite and professional athletes and teams are enthusiastically using mindfulness, because they have discovered that it enhances their performance and creates the conditions for finding flow.

Here's a short list of some of the athletes and teams that have used, or are using, mindfulness to enhance performance: the Los Angeles Lakers and the Chicago Bulls, the two most successful teams ever in the history of professional basketball, with multiple NBA championships between them; the New York Knicks; the Boston Red Sox; Shawn Green, multi-record-setting baseball player; Tim Lincecum, World Series pitcher for the San Francisco Giants; Derek Jeter, shortstop for the New York Yankees; the 2016 World Series–winning Chicago Cubs; Kerri Walsh-Jennings and Misty May-Trainor, Olympic beach volleyball gold medalists; Novak Djokovic, winner of twelve tennis Grand Slam titles; Sam Mikulak, US Olympic gymnast; the Baltimore Ravens; the Seattle Seahawks, 2015 NFL champions and 2016 runner-up; the US national BMX team, including 2016 Olympic gold medalist Connor Fields; and the Golden State Warriors, 2015 and 2017 NBA champions. In fact, the Warriors' declared core values are joy, mindfulness, compassion, and competition (Kawakami 2015).

So again, pause here and notice what you're thinking and feeling. Maybe you're thinking, *Cool! I'll give it a try.* Or maybe you're thinking, *This is weird. I doubt this will help me.* Whatever you're thinking or feeling is absolutely fine. There is nothing you need to change or fix. And I encourage you to keep reading, to actually *do* the practices in this book, and *then* choose for yourself what is helpful.

Finding Flow

As an athlete, you've *felt* it. That moment when time slows down and the world disappears, when even the sense of "you" as a separate self falls away and there is just movement, rhythm, energy, joy… That indescribable feeling is flow. Because the experience of flow is beyond the realm of thinking, it can never be fully expressed in words. The following quotes from Shawn Green, one of the all-time most accomplished players in Major League Baseball, and Harrison Barnes, from his time with the Golden State Warriors, come close to capturing the essence of flow:

> The truth is that while I was in the zone, I moved beyond the whole competition aspect of hitting. Absorbed in the act, it no longer mattered to me what team I was playing against or who was on the mound. There was only this: The ball came at me in slow motion, and I hit it. As the pitcher released the ball there was no me, no him,

no bat, and no ball. All nouns were gone, leaving only one verb: to hit. (Green 2011, 148)

I was in that flow state… You're out there moving, but you're not exerting any energy. You're shooting the ball, but you're not thinking if you're gonna miss or you're going to make it. You're just playing. The game is there. You're just letting it come to you naturally. (Abrams 2015)

In his book *Flow: The Psychology of Optimal Experience* (2009), pioneering flow researcher Mihaly Csikszentmihalyi defines nine qualities of flow. The qualities are listed below along with a personal example of gradually progressing from being a clumsy beginner to experiencing intermediate snowboarding flow. As you read you may want to reflect on your own cycles of developing flow—remember the first time you rode a bike without training wheels or a supportive hand, swam the width of a pool, skated rather than wobbled around a rink, or actually threw or caught a football.

Qualities of Flow

1. Skill-challenge balance: A situation in which you feel that you are being challenged *and* that you have the skills to meet the challenges. (*Anxiety*, when you feel you do not have the skills to meet the challenge, can be considered the opposite of flow.) When I was first learning to snowboard, I didn't have any skill or flow. Simply standing was challenging, as was maneuvering the board, getting on and off the lift, turning from heel side to toe side, and avoiding all the fixed and moving obstacles. My experience was one of awkwardness and moderate anxiety, definitely not flow.

2. Merging of action and awareness: A feeling of being at one with the activity; a sense of peace or harmony while performing an activity. At first, I was in my head, thinking about the instructions and *trying* to get my body to perform the movements described by my instructor. There was no sense of peace or harmony.

3. Clarity of purpose: A sense of feeling connected to the activity and of being able to respond skillfully in the moment. I didn't feel connected or in control of my board. I was not able to respond skillfully when I lost my balance or someone zoomed by.

4. Unambiguous (clear) feedback: The ability to effortlessly receive and process and respond to relevant information. Early on, I didn't even know what the relevant information was. I knew I preferred to be upright, but I didn't have a feel for how to interpret the feedback from the board, or how to move my body and the board in response to that feedback, to changes in terrain, to people, and to obstacles.

5. Concentration: Being completely focused on the activity in the present moment. Fortunately, thanks to a longtime mindfulness practice, I was able to concentrate on learning to snowboard.

6. Sense of control and confidence: An absence of fear of failure. I definitely did not have a sense of control and confidence. Because I was learning for fun, I didn't really have a fear of failure, though I was occasionally frustrated.

7. Loss of self-consciousness: Not worrying about "I," "me," and "my," or what others may be thinking about you and your performance. Even as a beginner, my mindfulness allowed me to be aware that I was self-conscious, that I wanted my instructor and classmates to think "I" was a "good student," "athletic," and a "quick learner."

8. Time transformation: When time slows, stops, or speeds up because you are fully engaged. Initially, time was just time; there was no sense of being out of time, or of being fully absorbed in the activity.

9. Autotelic experience: This is just a fancy way of saying that the experience is rewarding in and of itself, and not because you will win or get a spot on the roster. In short, this is truly *feeling* the love of the game.

Over time, I developed more skill and was able to meet increasing challenges. Now, even on intermediate runs I don't have to *think* about flexing my feet, directing my knees, shifting my weight, or keeping my shoulders in line with the board. I have a sense of peace and harmony. I am able to respond skillfully to changes in terrain and people and obstacles on the mountain. My body knows how to receive and respond to the feel of the board and the snow. While I concentrate, I can narrow and expand my field of awareness as needed. On intermediate terrain I have a sense of control and confidence. I am less worried about how I am doing and what others think. I have moments where I am just riding, out of time and space, and just moving and feeling the joy of flow. However, when I get on steeper terrain, into powder, or on bumps, the cycle of moving from awkwardness to flow begins all over again.

As we learn the skills of a sport, or the skills of mindfulness, we repeat this "moving from awkwardness to flow and then back to awkwardness cycle" many times as the level of challenge increases—moving to steeper terrain, bumping up a competitive level, adding more complex skills, increasing the degree of difficulty, and so forth.

As you will learn in "The Benefits of Mindfulness" section in chapter 2, scientific evidence demonstrates that practicing mindfulness can increase your ability to experience flow. My dear friend and colleague George Mumford, who taught mindfulness to Michael Jordan, Kobe Bryant, the championship Chicago Bulls, the Los Angeles Lakers, as well as many other elite and college athletes, clearly describes how the mind affects flow:

We can deconstruct the anatomy of flow in any way we want, but the truth of the matter is that it all starts in your mind. Flow is your ability to stay in the present moment… The real key to high performance and tapping into flow is the ability to direct and channel [your] strengths and skills fully in the present moment—and that starts in your mind. The flip side is also true. No matter how strong or skillful you might be, your mind can also impede talent from being expressed and it often does so in insidious ways if you don't take care of it. (2015, 69)

This book will help you become aware of patterns of thinking and feeling that negatively impact performance and, more importantly, will help you develop the essential mental, emotional, and spiritual skills that can enhance flow in sports and in life.

How to Use This Book

This book offers you essential skills for achieving peak performance and finding flow. Part 3 includes two related chapters for coaches and parents. Additional resources, including extra worksheets, related videos, and, most importantly, the downloadable audio recordings of practices, can be accessed at http://www.newharbinger.com/40217 (see the back of the book for information on how to access the downloads).

The essential skills in this book are presented in two parts: part 1, "The Fundamentals—Mindfulness," and part 2, "Advanced Skills—Integration." The exercises and principles build on each other, so it's best if you do them in order. The book begins with the basics and moves through specific intentional progressions toward the more complex, higher-level skills that will help you achieve peak performance and find flow in sports and in life. As with the physical fundamentals of any sport, it is best to work the basics before moving on to more challenging, higher-level skills. That said, if you find yourself curious about a particular topic, then flip to that page and learn what you can. Some of the sections later in the book build on earlier material, so I included cross-references to direct you to the earlier, relevant sections and chapters.

As you read, it may be helpful to know that the ellipsis (…) indicates a pause, a time to slow down and *really* allow yourself to *feel* or *experience* the full effect of the practices. Some phrases in this workbook will be repeated over and over so that eventually they live in your mind and heart and become a part of your life. Many themes will be presented several times in slightly different ways so that you can find what works best for you.

As an athlete, you may want to work with one chapter a week or a month. I suggest that you take your time, go slow, and allow yourself to really embody each element. To *embody* something means that it is alive inside of you—you feel it, live it, and express it in what you say, what you do, and who you are. You know it would be crazy to expect to execute any physical skill—a flawless flip turn or an ideally timed give-and-go—by just reading about it or listening to a coach explain it. It is the same for these mental and emotional skills. It is not enough to just read and think about these practices; to really benefit from these practices you must *do* them over and over until they live inside you and you can apply them in the heat of the moment.

There are four elements in this book:

Basic Concepts: As the name suggests, these sections present basic concepts that will support you in developing a comprehensive, personal mindfulness practice and using it to enhance your performance and find flow in sports and in life.

Practices: These elements will be the core of your mindfulness practice. You'll benefit from doing them *repeatedly*. So, for many of them I provide guided audio recordings, available at http://www.newharbinger.com/40217. Most of the athletes I work with load these recordings on their phones. That way they have the practices easily accessible when they want to use them—before a practice, tryout, or competition; to deal with a specific upset or challenge; or to just chill out.

Activities: These short, simple, paper-and-pencil and everyday activities will help you apply the concepts and practices in training, competition, and life. Some activities will encourage thoughtful contemplation. Others will have a playful quality.

Reflections: These sections will support you in integrating your experiences with the concepts, practices, and activities—as an athlete and as a human being. As you respond to the reflection prompts, I encourage you to go slowly and to be brave and specific. Do your best to discover what's true for you, how you *really* think, feel, and behave. The more *real* you can be with yourself, the more you will benefit.

In combination, the exercises in this book give you powerful skills for training your mind and heart, for facing common athletic challenges, and for becoming a master of the inner as well as the outer game. To repeat, the catch is that, just as with physical skills, developing these skills requires that you actually *do* the exercises.

As with physical skills, there may be some exercises that you find unusual or difficult, or even have serious doubts about. Over time, you may discover that the skills that you were initially most doubtful about, and found the most challenging, end up being the most useful, precisely because they helped you develop new and needed mental and emotional abilities. With patience, persistence, and a sense of humor, you will learn which practices are the most helpful to you and which you want to keep doing.

Notes

If you are an athlete who participates in an individual sport such as gymnastics, ice skating, swimming, track and field, wrestling, skiing, snowboarding, golf, or tennis, there may be some chapter elements, such as reading the game, that do not directly apply to your participation in your sport. That said, because most individual athletes train in team environments, go to school or work, and live in the company of others, most of the principles will likely be useful to you.

If your entire team is using this book together, it is essential that you promise to respect each other's privacy, and that all team members agree that if they happen to find someone else's book they will return it without opening it. This is a matter of trust, and trust is an essential element of teamwork and a healthy community.

And lastly, the online resources for this book provide additional helpful content, including audio downloads, extra copies of the worksheets, and links to videos of many of the performance scenarios described in the book. These resources are available at http://www.newharbinger.com/40217, and information about how to access them is in the back of the book.

CHAPTER 2

Taking a Rest, Taking a Breath

It is not possible to make flow happen at will…and attempting to do so will only make the state more elusive. However, removing obstacles and providing facilitating conditions will increase its occurrence. Learning the skills of mindfulness provides one way to facilitate the occurrence of flow.

—Susan Jackson

This chapter will briefly summarize the scientific evidence proving that mindfulness and related practices can help you find flow and perform at your best. It will also introduce you to the foundational practice of mindful resting.

Basic Concept: The Benefits of Mindfulness

This section simplifies and summarizes the current scientific research proving that mindfulness improves performance and enhances flow. I chose to highlight a few studies and provide a table summarizing the research to date. Because the studies vary in design and the specific measures used, the list of benefits includes interrelated definitions, such as stress and psychological distress. If you are interested, a more detailed summary of the studies and results ("Review of the Research") is included with the online resources (visit http://www.newharbinger.com/40217).

- Olympic rowers who medaled reported that mindfulness practice had helped them prepare for and achieve optimal performance. College rowers who participated in mindfulness training performed well above the expectations of their coach and said the training had enhanced their concentration, relaxation, and synchronicity of technique, while reducing the impact of their fatigue, pain, and negative thoughts (Kabat-Zinn, Beall, and Rippe 1985).

- Cyclists who participated in an eight-week mindfulness intervention, with a mindful spin-bike component, showed increases in mindfulness and flow and decreases in pessimism (Scott-Hamilton, Schutte, and Brown 2016).

- Junior elite soccer players who took part in a seven-session program based on the mindfulness, acceptance, and commitment approach had almost half the number of injuries of the control group (Ivarsson et al. 2015)!

- In a four-week study with elite male shooters, the mindfulness group showed a significant reduction in salivary cortisol (major stress hormone) and a significant improvement in shooting performance (John, Verma, and Khanna 2011).

- Young elite golfers who were taught mindfulness and acceptance improved the effectiveness of their training and their competitive performance, as measured by higher national ranking (Bernier et al. 2009).

- A functional magnetic resonance imaging (fMRI) study showed that members of the US national BMX team who participated in a seven-week mindfulness performance enhancement, awareness, and knowledge (mPEAK) training experienced changes in activity in specific regions of the brain, reflecting an increased ability to perform optimally under extreme stress (Haase et al. 2015).

In summary, the previous studies and related research show that athletes who are naturally mindful, or who practice mindfulness, experience both reductions and increases in a number of performance-related phenomena (see the following lists).

Reductions

- Stress
- Precompetition stress
- Psychological distress
- Salivary cortisol (major stress hormone)
- Sports anxiety
- Negative thoughts
- Task-related worries
- Task-irrelevant thoughts
- Rumination (obsessive thinking)

- Pessimism
- Depression
- Perfectionism
- Fatigue
- Pain
- Hostility
- Eating concerns
- Substance use
- Injury
- Burnout

Increases

- Mindfulness
- Flow
- Relaxation
- Confidence
- Clear goals
- Goal-directed energy
- Sports-related optimism
- Ability to act with awareness
- Concentration
- Ability to focus attention and ignore distractions
- Sense of control
- Ability to acknowledge and accept feelings
- Adaptive emotion regulation
- Psychological flexibility
- Resilience (the ability to bounce back)
- Ability to pay attention to the body
- Effectiveness of training
- Ability to anticipate and recover from an intense physical challenge
- Ability to perform optimally under extreme stress (as shown with fMRI brain imaging)
- Sleep quality
- Physical recovery
- Ability to perform well above the expectations of the coach
- Game free-throw percentage of 5.75
- Synchronicity of technique
- Competitive performance, as measured against best performance the previous year and by improved national ranking
- Appreciation of the process (not just the outcome) of competition
- Enjoyment of the sport
- General life satisfaction

The take-home message is this: just as physical training strengthens the body, mindfulness training strengthens the mind and spirit. So if you want your mind and spirit to be better able to deal with the stresses of training, competition, and daily life, keep reading and practicing, starting with the practice below.

Practice: Rest

This first practice will allow you to just rest and chill out for a few minutes. It is a short and simple way to take a break from the challenges of sports, school, work, and life. A downloadable audio recording of this practice is available at http://www.newharbinger.com/40217. You may want to take a few minutes right now to download all the recorded practices, including this one, so you can simply close your eyes and listen to each practice when you come to it. If you're choosing to learn this practice by reading it, you may want to read a paragraph, then close your eyes and slowly follow the instructions in that paragraph, then read the next paragraph, and so on. As you read and practice, let the feeling of rest wash over you.

It will be helpful to find a protected place where you won't be disturbed—a quiet corner of the locker room, outside on a bench or by a tree, or in your bedroom. Once you become more familiar with mindful resting, you'll be able to do it anywhere—before a tryout, in a busy airport, between events at a meet or games at a tournament, or after an exciting win or a rough loss.

Give it a rest. For the next few minutes, give it a rest—all of it—today's practice, tomorrow's competition, school, work, friendships, family, the hallway gossip, your inner gossip, the next new thing.... Let everything be exactly the way it is...and rest.

Let your body rest. If you feel comfortable, allow your eyes to close. If not, focus on a neutral spot in front of you. Feel your body supported by the locker room bench, hotel couch, or your bed. Allow the muscles in your body and your face to rest. Maybe even let out a long, slow sigh....

Let your attention rest on the breath...the rhythm of the breath in the belly. Feel the belly expand with each in-breath and release with each out-breath...narrowing your attention to the rhythm of the breath and allowing everything else to fade into the background.... Breathing, resting.... Nowhere to go, nothing to do, no one to be, nothing to prove.

Feel the entire in-breath, from the very first sip all the way through to where the breath is still...and the entire out-breath, from the first whisper all the way through to where the breath is still.... Now see if you can let your attention rest in the Still Quiet Place between the in-breath and the out-breath.... And rest again in the still space between the out-breath and the in-breath...

Breathing, resting, being.... This is more than enough...just hanging out with the breath and the stillness....

Feeling the stillness and quietness that are always inside of you....

And when your attention wanders, which it will, gently return it to the experience of breathing—feeling the rhythm of the breath in the belly....

Choosing to rest. Choosing to focus your attention on the breath. Allowing things to be just as they are...allowing yourself to be exactly as you are.... There's nothing to change, or fix, or improve....

Breathing and resting. Resting and breathing.

As this practice session comes to a close, you may want to remember that in our fast-paced media-driven world, resting is a radical act. With practice, you can learn to breathe and rest anytime, anywhere: when you're lacing up your cleats...when you're struggling in class or practice...when you're hanging out with friends...when things aren't going your way.... This kind of resting and breathing is especially helpful when you're feeling nervous, frustrated, excited, or angry. And just like with physical skills, the more you practice, the more natural this skill will become. So commit to practicing breathing and resting in stillness and quietness. And remember, you can return to stillness and quietness any time you want simply by resting your attention on the breath.

Now that you have finished reading, please *give yourself permission to rest* by either listening to the recorded audio or simply resting with your breath for three to five minutes, as described.

Reflection: What Was It Like to Rest?

Take some time to reflect on your experience of resting and answer the following questions.

Were you able to rest? Circle one: Yes.   No.   Sort of.

Whether you were able to rest or not, bring your kind and curious attention to your experience by answering the following questions.

How did your mind feel? _____

_____

How did your body feel? _____

_____

How did your heart feel? _____

_____

What helped you rest? _____

_____

What did you find challenging about resting? _____

_____

Because most of us are used to being on the go and thinking about all the things we have to do, resting may feel like a huge relief, or it may feel unusual or even uncomfortable. However you experienced resting is *absolutely fine*. With practice, resting in stillness and quietness will become easier.

Sometimes when you sit down to rest, you may discover that your mind is racing, that you're feeling sad or angry, or that your body is fidgety. Noticing these experiences with kindness and curiosity *is* mindfulness. Images on social media, in the movies, on TV, and on magazine covers give the impression that being mindful means always being calm, peaceful, and blissed out. It doesn't! Being mindful means simply being aware of whatever is happening here and now. So if your body is exhausted, your mood is excited, or your mind is bored, and you're aware of your experience, you're being mindful.

Again, there's nothing you need to change or fix. It's more than enough to simply bring your kind and curious attention to your experience in the moment, here and now. George Mumford, mindfulness coach for the Chicago Bulls, Los Angeles Lakers, New York Knicks, and other elite athletes, highlights the benefit of this deep connection to the present moment in the context of athletics and life:

> The more deeply connected we are to the vastness of our own still, quiet center, the less thrown off balance we are by whatever distractions and challenges come our way. (2015, 82)

Activity: Bowing In and Bowing Out

When I was a young gymnast, my coach was very interested in the training techniques of male Japanese gymnasts. At the time, the Japanese men dominated international competition. My coach had visited Japan, and he brought home an extremely simple yet powerful tool. He asked us to bow when we entered the gym.

This simple action indicated that we were leaving everything—homework, friends, family, romance (or lack thereof), social events, joys, and upsets—outside the gym, and we were committing to being fully present and engaged during practice. In *The Inner Game of Tennis*, Tim Gallwey notes that mastering this type of focused attention can be more valuable than mastering a particular athletic skill:

> If, while learning tennis, you begin to learn how to focus your attention and how to trust in yourself, you have learned something far more valuable than how to hit a forceful backhand. The backhand can be used to advantage only on a tennis court, but the skill of mastering the art of effortless concentration is invaluable in whatever you set your mind to. (2008, 8)

Below, jot down a brief description of a simple action you can do mindfully to bring yourself fully into the present moment at the beginning of practice. The action doesn't need to be a bow; it could be a mindful nod of the head, a jump into the pool, or a step onto the ice.

_____

_____

_____

When we completed practice, my coach also had us bow out. I did this so many times during my competitive years that thirty-six years later I can still sense the gym just as it was: the blue floor-exercise mat illuminated by fluorescent lights; the sounds of the participants in the late-night recreational classes adjusting the bars or sticking a landing; the musty chalk dust in the air; and the cool (often freezing in Colorado) late-night air that greeted me as I bowed, pushed the door open with my back, and left the gym. This simple action of bowing out symbolized that, for better or worse, that day's workout was complete.

Together bowing in and bowing out marked practice time as a specific time devoted to cultivating excellence. Knowing and acknowledging when practice begins and when it ends allows us to bring our best to our training sessions.

Below, jot down a brief description of a simple mindful action you can do to close your practice. Again, it doesn't need to be a bow; it could be tossing the last ball into the bucket, taking off your helmet, or zipping up your gear bag.

_____

_____

_____

Practice: Between Bowing In and Bowing Out

While bowing in and bowing out mark practice as a specific time for cultivating excellence, it is important to be able to return your focus to the task at hand within a given practice or competition. So just like during the Rest practice above, when you notice your mind has wandered during training, simply return your attention to the moment, to your breath, to your body, to the specifics of the environment—the feel of your feet on the ground or your hand in the mitt. Adam Kreek, a Canadian rower who won Olympic gold in 2008, believes

> that the conscious presence in each moment is the golden key to effective practice. Practice is not about going through the motions with our body while our mind and spirit reside elsewhere. Rather, practice is about focused effort with our entire being. This engrains habit and skill into our unconscious self. The goal of being in the now during practice is to create an unconscious competence within our mind, body, and spirit. (Afremow 2013, 191)

Activity: Pleasant Events

Often we are so busy, in our heads, and focused on our problems that we don't notice the pleasant events in our lives—simple moments of ease, happiness, and fun. See if you can remember a pleasant event from the last couple of days.

Social media, TV, and advertising tell us that pleasant events have to be big, exciting, and sexy, like going to a cool party, getting an amazing gift, or winning the state championship. Yet pleasant events are often short, simple, and sweet: petting your dog, nailing a difficult shot at the end of practice, laughing with a friend, solving a math problem, rocking out to your favorite song, seeing a beautiful sunset…

Once you've remembered a pleasant event, fill in the following page. Just a few brief words or sketches are fine. In the Thought Bubble, note the thoughts that appeared during the pleasant event. In the Feelings Bubble, note the emotions that appeared during the event. And in the Body Bubble, note what was happening in your body and how your body felt during the event.

As you fill in the page, it may be helpful to consider your five senses—sight, hearing, taste, touch, and smell—as well as the facial expressions and body sensations you experienced during the pleasant event.

If you're having difficulty remembering something pleasant, *think small*. Did you hear a great new song or a funny joke? As you walked to practice, could you feel the sunshine or the breeze on your face? Did you share an easy moment with a teammate? Did you enjoy a delicious sandwich?

PLEASANT EVENT

Event: _____

Thought Bubble

Feelings Bubble

Body Bubble

PLEASANT EVENTS CALENDAR

Day: What was the event?	What thoughts appeared during the event?	What feelings or emotions appeared during the event?	How did your body feel during the event?	What thoughts, feelings, and body sensations are present now, as you write about the event?
Monday:				
Tuesday:				
Wednesday:				

Thursday:	Friday:	Saturday:	Sunday:

You may wonder what the point of this exercise is. Appreciating the pleasant events in our lives brings us into the present moment and is a great antidote to stress. For survival, our minds are trained to look for problems and threats. When our distant ancestors were living in the wild, in the jungle or on the savanna, this was very helpful. However, these days this mental habit stresses most of us out because our minds mistakenly interpret ordinary daily experiences (losing a cell phone, having a rough practice, or getting tough feedback from a teammate or a coach) as life-threatening events. When our minds do this, our bodies react and produce stress hormones, creating a low level of panic.

To balance out the mind's tendency to engage in *negative scanning*, or looking for threats, and to simply enjoy our lives more, it helps to practice appreciating the pleasant moments in our lives. And appreciating pleasant events lays a solid foundation for a more advanced gratitude practice, described in chapter 12.

Giving Yourself the Gift of Mindfulness

For the next week or so, try the following:

- Do the Rest practice at least once a day, preferably by listening to the downloadable audio recording. Most athletes find that the best times to listen are after school or work, before practice, between homework subjects, or before bed. Do your best to create a routine that works for you.

- Create your own rituals to begin and end athletic practice.

- Practice positive scanning throughout the day. At the end of each day, write down at least one simple pleasant moment. You might set up a daily reminder on your phone and use the pleasant events calendar in this chapter to record these events and how you respond. Interestingly, committing to writing down a pleasant event at the end of each day often helps us be more aware of pleasant events throughout the day.

Remember, learning mindfulness and positive scanning (recognizing and appreciating the pleasant events in your life, as well as your own progress and developing athletic abilities), is like mastering athletic skills. The more you practice, the more skilled you'll become.

CHAPTER 3

Bringing Awareness to the Body

The more awareness one can bring to bear on any action, the more feedback one gets from experience, and the more naturally one learns.

—Tim Gallwey

In this chapter you will play with bringing your kind and curious attention to your body, as it rests in stillness, performs the basics of your warm-up and cooldown routines, and completes the more complex movements of practice and competition. The principles in this chapter will help you develop your ability to be aware of both obvious and subtle sensations in the body.

Mindfulness of the body can be extremely helpful in three specific ways: (1) it can help you fine-tune your performance, (2) it can help you really check in and see where you are physically, and (3) it can help you be in the moment, right here, right now, and not stuck in your head obsessing about the future or the past.

Basic Concept: Mindfulness of the Body

The ability to *feel* the body is essential for optimal athletic performance. As an athlete, it is critical to develop *proprioception*, the ability to sense the body's position, equilibrium, and motion. Proprioception allows you to feel the subtle adjustments in weight, balance, power, trajectory, and timing that make the difference between a quick, powerful start off the blocks and a slower, sluggish one; between completing the triple Salchow and landing on your backside; between the three-pointer that goes swish and the one that bounces off the rim. Bringing awareness to physical sensations using the Body Scan and Stretch and Balance practice (audio recordings are included with the online resources available at http://www.newharbinger.com /40217) and, ultimately, during training and competition, enhances proprioception; enhanced proprioception allows you to naturally receive your body's real-time feedback and fine-tune your execution. Ultimately, this type of body awareness will help you experience flow.

Throughout his book *The Way of Baseball: Finding Stillness at 95 MPH*, Shawn Green offers many detailed descriptions of the truly game-changing process of shifting attention from the mind to the body while batting:

> The work consisted of my swinging in a place of no thought, learning to peel my awareness away from my mind and redirect it into my body…
>
> I discovered that the space existed at a midpoint between the coiling of my body and the unraveling of that position. It is similar to the movement of breathing. There is a slight pause between an inhalation and an exhalation…
>
> All the power in my swing arose out of that empty space… Though lasting only a fraction of a second, the space sometimes felt like an eternity, making a ninety-five miles per hour fastball seem to float in like a beach ball. (2011, 32)

This type of nuanced body awareness not only allows you to refine your performance, but it also helps you develop *interoception*, the ability to feel the body from the inside out. Interoception is important for preventing overtraining and overuse injuries. With experience, you can learn to distinguish typical fatigue from the deep exhaustion of overtraining, and the normal aches and pains of training from the more serious stabs and twinges of true injury. In fact, as previously mentioned, a research study with elite soccer players from Sweden found that athletes who practiced mindfulness had fewer injuries (Ivarsson et al. 2015).

Combining mindful body awareness with training logs documenting workout type, time, intensity, and other sport-specific measurements will help you find the optimal balance between high-intensity training and equally necessary rest and recovery (see "Periodization" in chapter 4). Examples of sport-specific measurements include routine repetitions in skating and gymnastics, pitch counts and speeds in baseball, power output in cycling, minutes played, and sophisticated analyses of micromovements (acceleration, change in direction, applied force, and biomechanical load) detected by cutting-edge sensors used by many professional sports teams (Leung 2015). Ultimately, mindful awareness of your body can help you maximize your physical abilities and simultaneously be aware of, and honor, your body's limits.

Practice: Body Scan

You can download an audio recording of this practice at http://www.newharbinger.com/40217.

So let's practice bringing kind attention to the body. Sit or lie in a comfortable position. If you feel comfortable, allow your eyes to close, or if not, then focus on a neutral spot in front of you.

Allow your arms to rest by your sides, and if your legs are crossed, uncross them.

On the next in-breath, feel your back lengthen and straighten. On the next out-breath, allow your muscles to soften. And take a moment to check in with your body. How is your body, in this moment?... What is your overall energy level?... Are there any areas requesting your kind and curious attention?... Are there any signs of impending injury or illness, or of recovery and improving health?...

In your own time, bring your attention to the familiar expansion and release of the breath in the belly. Let your attention rest on the rhythm of the breath. To help yourself pay attention to the breath, you may want to place one hand on your belly and the other on your chest... feeling the rhythm of the breath, and noticing how your body, mind, and heart responded to this simple touch....

When you are ready, let your hands rest in your lap or at your sides, and breathe your kind and curious attention into your feet. Notice the sensations in your feet—the feel of your socks, your shoes, or, if you are barefoot, the feel of the air.

Perhaps you can be aware of the spaces between your toes? Perhaps you can feel the sensations in the muscles and bones of your feet?

Now, allow the breath and the attention to move up into the ankles and lower legs. Noting the sensations in the ankles, and feeling the curve of the calf muscles and straightness of the shinbones....

When you are ready, breathe your attention into the knees. Feeling the muscles and tendons that move and support the knees, and then feeling into the knee joints....

Breathing and feeling the sensations in the knees, and perhaps noticing any experiences that happen to be here, now—ease, restlessness, peace, sleepiness, irritation.... Letting it all be, just as it is.

And in your own time, breathing the attention into the backs of your thighs and buttocks, feeling the places where your legs make contact with the chair, the floor, or the bed, and the places where they don't. Allowing the attention to circle around the outer thighs, up, over the tops of the thighs, and across the inner thighs. Perhaps you can feel the weight of your clothing and the specific sensations in the different areas of the thighs.

And now, breathing your attention into the bowl of your pelvis, the place where your legs connect with your body. Perhaps you can feel the breath expanding and releasing in the bowl of your pelvis.

Now, again, focusing your attention on the familiar rising and falling of the breath in your belly. Resting deeply in the stillness and quietness between the in-breaths and the out-breaths, and underneath the breath....

Allow the breath and attention to sink through the belly into the low back. See if you can feel the breath expanding and releasing in the low back. Experiment with simply noticing what is happening in your body, sensations of tension, comfort, or perhaps neutrality, which is a kind of nothingness. Play with noticing your experience without any judgment or story.

Now, let the breath and the attention move upward into the mid and upper back, feeling the breath in the mid and upper back, exploring the region between the shoulder blades....

When your attention is pulled by a thought or feeling, or a more involved story, gently, kindly, return your attention to the instructions.

When you are ready, allow the breath and attention to circle around the rib cage into the chest, feeling the movement and sensations of the breath in the chest.

Now, letting the breath and attention drift up into the shoulders, and down along the length of your arms into your hands. Noting any sensations of ache, strength, and comfort in the arms. Exploring the sensations in the palms of the hands and the backs of the hands, the fingers and thumbs.

And now moving the breath and attention into the neck, feeling along the back of the neck, the sides of the neck, and the front of the neck. Perhaps even feeling the movement of the breath in the throat.

Now, allow the breath and the attention to move up into your face, feeling the position of your jaw, the curve of your lips, and your facial expression.

Perhaps you can feel the breath moving in and out at the tip of your nose; the sensations in the cheeks, eyes, and eyelids; and the touch of your hair, or the air on your forehead?

Let the breath and attention circle along the sides of the head, into the ears, to the back of the head, up to the top of the head, and into the brain....

Now let breath and attention fill your entire body—brain, head, face, neck, arms, hands, chest, back, belly, pelvis, legs, and feet.

Feel the breath filling you and emptying you. If you wish, you can play with breathing the breath up from the bottom of your feet; through your legs, torso, arms, neck, and head; and back down from your head through your neck, arms torso, legs, and feet—like sipping the breath up, and releasing the breath down through your body like liquid in a straw.

Take a moment to appreciate the stillness and quietness, energy and aliveness inside of you, and to be grateful for this body, this one that is here right now, exactly as it is....

And as this session comes to an end, it can be helpful to remember that bringing your kind and curious attention to the body can help you tune in to your body, and come home to yourself, especially in difficult moments. Any time you find yourself stuck in obsessive thinking, or upset by intense feelings, you can bring your attention to the body in very short, simple, secret ways. You can notice the sensations of breathing, your feet on the ground.... Often, choosing to drop your attention out of your head and into your body—your belly, or your feet—can decrease the intensity of obsessive thinking and feeling.

Being mindful of the body is one way to drop into the moment, into the Still Quiet Place, into flow.

Reflection: Body Scan

What was it like to bring your attention to your body?

_____

_____

_____

_____

What did you discover about how your body is in this moment?

_____

_____

_____

_____

How do your mind and heart feel, now that you have given your body some kind and curious attention?

_____

_____

_____

_____

Activity: Finger Yoga

Place your left hand on your left thigh. *Gently* use your right index and middle finger to pull the fourth finger on your left hand backward. Notice your limit—the place where you need to stop pulling to avoid causing pain or injury.

The purpose of this very simple exercise is for you to practice *really* listening to your body, fully stretching to your current limit, and then backing off a bit when things get too intense.

Now perhaps you can consider doing some other simple stretches with the same level of kind and curious attention. For example, stand and stretch both arms up overhead and then lean from your waist in an arc to the right, creating a C shape with your body and feeling the sensations of the stretch, the breath expanding the ribs on the left, the compression on the right… Then repeat the stretch on the other side, leaning to the left… As you stretch, breathe naturally and bring your kind and curious attention to the *experience* of stretching.

For another stretch, stand and clasp your hands together behind your back. Then gently raise your arms up behind you as high as you can while keeping your body vertical, your chest up, feeling the sensations in your chest, shoulders, and arms. Notice how your body, mind, and heart feel after bringing your full attention to doing these simple stretches. (A slightly longer, more complete, downloadable audio recording of the Stretch and Balance practice can be found with this book's online resources at http://www.newharbinger.com/40217.)

With practice, you can learn to gently stretch into discomfort, not only in your body but also in your mind and heart. For example, if you have a challenging team situation or an emotional upset, you can experiment with stretching and easing into your frustration or sadness. Maybe you can try just *being* with your frustration or sadness for three full breaths?

We will explore this more in chapter 6, "Befriending Feelings." For now it may be helpful to know that, as with physical stretching, you can practice gently stretching into mental and emotional experiences. As with physical stretching, when you stretch mentally and emotionally, it is important to know when to back off, release, and ask for help. And just like when you stretch your body, when you stretch your mind and heart, they become more flexible and more balanced.

Practice: Embodied Warm-Ups and Cooldowns

After practicing the Body Scan, paying attention to the body when it is still, you can begin to incorporate mindful body awareness into your practices, by warming up or cooling down, mindfully, in silence, two or three times a week. As you move through your usual skills and stretches, let all the thoughts and feelings of the day drift into the background, and bring your full attention to your body—really *feel* the tone of your muscles, the stiffness or flexibility of your joints, your energy level, your heart rate, and your breathing. However your body is today is fine; there is no need to change anything. It is enough to simply bring your full attention to becoming aware of your body as it is in this moment.

Activity: Seeing and Feeling—Visualize and Body-ize

Improving a particular element of your sport by observing elite athletes and through visualization are distinct skills. Although they don't always use the term "mindfulness," experts such as Jim Taylor, a well-known sports psychologist, suggest that these skills are most powerful when they are mindfully embodied. *Mindfully embodied* means not just watching elite athletes, or envisioning yourself performing a specific move, but actually *feeling* yourself doing the movement.

> Good imagery is more than just visual, that's why I don't like to call it visualization. The best imagery involves the multi-sensory reproduction of the actual sport experience. You should duplicate the sights, sounds, physical sensations, thoughts, and emotions that you would experience in an actual competition… The most powerful part of mental imagery is feeling it in your body. That's how you really ingrain new technical and mental skills and habits. A useful way to increase the feeling in your mental imagery is to combine imagined and real sensations. Imagine yourself performing and move your body along with the imagery. (Taylor 2012)

This week choose one simple, very specific element of your sport that you want to improve—for example, the last step and lift for a layup; the stance, weight distribution, and angle of an effective tackle; the depth and trajectory of entry for a starting dive in swimming. Google videos of the best in the world doing this element, and as you watch the videos see if you can *feel* your body doing the element. Or better yet, watch videos of your best performance of the element. Then close your eyes and see and feel yourself successfully doing the element, from the inside out.

Please keep in mind that watching and feeling the movement of the pros can indeed be helpful, and it is important to note that every body is different, and what works well for a pro of a certain height, weight, power, and flexibility may not be most effective for you. Putting your attention fully into *your* body and *feeling* your way through will allow you to discover what works best for you. As you continue to use the practices in this book, you may want to choose a particular skill every week to see and feel, or to *visualize* and *body-ize*.

Perhaps one of the most incredible athletic feats attributable to embodied visualization is Stanford wide-receiver Francis Owusu's behind-the-back touchdown catch. The catch, made during Stanford's 2015 regular-season 56–35 win over UCLA, was dubbed "catch of the year." To be clear, Owusu didn't catch the football behind his back—he caught it behind his opponent's back. Even though he couldn't see the ball, Owusu reached around his opponent, gave him a bear hug, caught the ball while both players were falling, and managed to hold on to it.

Much of the credit goes to Owusu's coach, who created a drill in which the receiver's vision was blurred during plays. As Osuwu noted, "For that split second, you gotta track it, see where it's gonna land and you just gotta mentally prepare for it" (Mazeika 2015).

Practice: Breathing Into and Through

You can combine the practices of breathing and feeling your body in motion during practice and competition. My friend and colleague Todd Corbin is a Little League coach, and he encourages his players to breathe (and feel) through a pitch, a swing, or a throw. Shawn Green writes, "One conscious breath can relax the body, whether at bat, at the free-throw line, in the middle of a contentious business meeting, driving on the freeway, or talking through a relationship issue" (2011, 121). Where can you breathe into or through an element of your sport? The free throw? The penalty kick? The last tumbling pass?

_____

_____

Activity: Outward as Well as Inward

It is obviously valuable to turn our attention inward, to check in with our body, to see how we are feeling, and to use this information to adjust our training, our diets, our sleep, and specific elements of our sport. Bringing this same type of kind and curious attention to external conditions can also be beneficial. For many sports it is useful to be aware of the weather—is it hotter or cooler than usual? How strong is the wind and what direction is it blowing? Relatively speaking, is the competitive surface fast or slow? Is the ref being lax, or calling everything? Is your teammate on fire, or a bit slower than usual? Does your opponent tend to move to the left, or to the right? Andre Agassi, winner of multiple Grand Slam titles, offers a vivid example of the benefits of this type of outward attention. By paying attention to Boris Becker's tongue, Agassi figured out Becker's "tell" and improved his ability to compete with Becker: "Just before he tosses the ball, Becker sticks out his tongue and it points like a tiny red arrow to where he's aiming" (2009).

Being aware of subtle and not-so-subtle details regarding the external conditions allows you to make necessary adjustments. If it is hot you can drink more. If it is windy, or the surface is slow, you can put a little more power into a soccer pass or a backhand. If the ref is calling everything, you can play really clean. If your opponent is playing to the left, you can shift your position. If your teammate is a bit off, you can slow the pass or pass to someone else.

Practice: Seeing Space and Opportunity

While many young athletes only focus on making the pass or the shot, more experienced and skillful athletes also learn to see space. Like finding the still quiet place between breaths, you can expand your perception to include space—the open spaces on the court or field, the spaces between defenders, the spaces you or your teammates might move into, the spaces in which you pause or accelerate. Seeing space allows for tremendous creativity, possibility, and opportunity. Can you practice seeing and feeling space—for yourself, your teammates, the ball, or the puck?

The next time you have the opportunity to walk somewhere crowded—a busy street, a subway station, an airport—practice quick, mindful walking. Feel the movements of your body, your feet making contact with the ground, your legs striding, your arms swinging, your breath. And practice seeing, not just the people and the objects in the environment, but the space between the people and the objects. This space is like the still quiet place between breaths, the pause between thoughts, the peace between feelings. And, of course, when you are ready, you can take this practice to the field, the court, or the ice.

Giving Yourself the Gift of Mindfulness

For the next week or so, try the following:

- Alternate listening to the Body Scan and the Stretch and Balance practices (audio recordings are available with the online resources at http://www.newharbinger.com /40217).

- Practice bringing your kind and curious attention inward to your body and outward to the environment.

- Use transitions and pauses in play during practice and competition to return your attention to the here and now—to your body, the environment, your opponent, and your teammates as they are in this moment.

- Choose one skill to visualize and body-ize.

- Play with seeing space and opportunity.

CHAPTER 4

Self-Care

*To know what your body wants…to understand what it needs and what it doesn't, you
need to be part engineer, part mathematician, part artist, part mystic*

—Gil Reyes, Andre Agassi's trainer

This chapter offers basic information about mindfully caring for your body while training and
during competition. The US Olympic Committee's motto, "It is not every four years, it is every
day," clearly suggests that day-to-day choices create excellence. Jim Afremow, author of *The
Champion's Mind: How Great Athletes Think, Train, and Thrive*, writes, "You do not need to be
disciplined every second of the day. You only need to be disciplined for those few key moments
during the day when you need to avoid temptation and/or start a positive action" (2013, 15).
Together these two quotes highlight a balanced approach to self-care and achieving peak performance. As noted, no one can be mindful and disciplined every moment. And it is important to be able to recognize key moments, and to make choices in those moments that will
support your development as an athlete. In this chapter you will consider many of the basic
choices you make regarding your physical health, training, and competition.

Basic Concept: Fine-Tuning

Although you can't control everything, and things don't always go as planned, it is important
to bring your kind and curious attention to all aspects of your health and well-being, and to
learn what works best for you during both training and competition. You may be fortunate to
have a coach, like my first gymnastics coach, who is devoted to learning and sharing everything
he can about optimizing your potential, or you may have an old-school coach who coaches the
way she was coached despite good science suggesting other methods might be better. In the

long run, it is up to you to learn from coaches, nutritionists, trainers, sport-specific articles and books, and, most importantly, your own body, to develop and refine the systems and routines that allow you to perform at your best.

The following sections summarize some of the basic science related to fine-tuning athletic performance and provide prompts to support you in developing habits to improve your physical health and optimize your ability to train and compete.

Sleep

Scientific research confirms common sense: getting extra sleep improves specific, measurable performance parameters, mood, and alertness (American Academy of Sleep Medicine 2008). Basketball players who added two hours of sleep and slept a minimum of ten hours measurably improved their on-court performance—specifically sprint speed, and both free-throw and three-point percentages by 9 percent. The players also reported decreased feelings of tension, anger, and confusion during practices and games (Mah et al. 2011). Swimmers who extended their sleep reacted 0.15 second quicker off the blocks, swam a 15-meter sprint 0.51 second faster, improved turn time by 0.10 second, and increased kick strokes by 5 kicks (American Academy of Sleep Medicine 2008).

Cheri Mah, a researcher at the Stanford Center for Sleep Sciences and Medicine and lead author of both of the previously referenced studies, writes, "Athletes across all sports can greatly benefit from extra sleep and gain the additional competitive edge to perform at their highest level... Many of the athletes in the various sports I have worked with...have set multiple new personal records and season best times, as well as broken long-standing Stanford and American records (American Academy of Sleep Medicine 2008).

So with this in mind, bring your kind and curious attention to your sleep habits, filling in the blanks or circling the appropriate answer.

What time do you usually go to sleep? _____

What time do you usually wake up? _____

How well do you sleep?   Great.   Okay.   Not so great.

Are you getting at least ten hours of quality sleep a night?   Yes.   No.

Knowing that athletes usually perform best with at least ten hours
of quality sleep, do you need more high-quality sleep?   Yes.   No.

If yes, how might you adjust your schedule to get more sleep?

_____

_____

_____

What habits will you need to change to get more sleep? Do you need to spend less time on social media, watching TV, hanging out with friends or teammates? Should you avoid drinking caffeinated beverages after 3 p.m?

Other: _____

Interestingly, people with insomnia who practice mindfulness report sleeping better, waking more refreshed, feeling less distressed about insomnia, and being better able to cope when it occurs (Hubbling et al. 2014).

Nutrition

Your body will function best if you eat natural foods—fruits, vegetables, whole grains, lean meats, milk, cheese, and eggs—and avoid processed foods. Processed foods are often white, such as white flour and white sugar, and contain added fats, sugars (ingredients ending with "ose," such as sucrose, fructose, and dextrose), salt, and artificial ingredients. Prepackaged foods are more likely to be highly processed. Multiple ingredients with names you don't recognize suggest the food is processed. You will also want to avoid foods that don't sit well in your system due to a true food allergy or food intolerance. If you suspect you have a food allergy or food intolerance because you frequently feel bloated, gassy, and achy after eating a particular food, you can test your theory by following an allergy-elimination diet during a rest-and-recovery period.

Considering the very basic information above, for at least the next week bring your kind and curious attention to what you eat, how you eat, how much you eat, and how your body feels after you eat. Then answer these questions by filling in the blanks or circling the correct response.

Is the majority of the food you eat natural or processed?

Do you include a healthy balance of fruits and vegetables, high-quality protein
(lean meats, eggs, dairy, nuts, beans), carbohydrates (whole-grain breads and
pastas, brown rice, potatoes), and healthy fats (olive oil, avocado oil)?   Yes.   No.

Do you have general sense of how many calories you are eating and burning?	Yes.	No.
Can you recognize signs of hunger (emptiness in your belly, slight headache, fatigue, irritability, inability to complete a workout)?	Yes.	No.
Can you recognize signs of satiety, when your body is satisfied because you have eaten enough but not too much food (the feeling of a 75 percent full belly, mental clarity, sufficient energy)?	Yes.	No.
Do you eat when you are hungry and stop slightly before you are full?	Yes.	No.
Do you turn to food for comfort when you are angry, tired, or lonely?	Yes.	No.

And if so, what do you tend to crave?

_____

_____

Hydration

Proper hydration is another essential element of optimal performance. It is well known that dehydration negatively affects the performance of athletes competing in distance events, such as running, cycling, and triathlons. Research shows that exercise performance is impaired when an individual is dehydrated by as little as 2 percent of body weight, and losses in excess of 5 percent of body weight can decrease performance capacity by about 30 percent. It is less well known that dehydration prior to performing high-intensity (sprint type) exercise, which results in exhaustion within a few minutes, also affects performance. If an athlete is dehydrated by 2.5 percent of body weight, her performance capacity can be reduced by as much as 45 percent (Jeukendrup and Gleeson 2010).

Thus, it is essential that you practice hydration basics. Proper hydration is even more important when you are traveling, because travel itself is dehydrating, and it is especially important when you are training and competing in hot or humid climates, or both, and at altitude. To get a sense of your typical level of hydration, answer these questions by filling in the blanks or circling the correct response.

Are you drinking six to eight glasses of water per day?	Yes.	No.
Are you drinking fewer than two caffeinated beverages (soda, coffee) per day?	Yes.	No.

(Caffeine is dehydrating. Even though soda and coffee are liquid, they actually make you produce urine and pee out more fluid than you take in. This is also the case with alcohol. So from a hydration perspective, if you are going to consume caffeine or alcohol you want to increase your noncaffeinated fluid intake.)

Is your urine a very light yellow?   Yes.   No.

(Bringing your kind and curious attention to the color of your urine is a simple way to determine whether you are hydrated. Ideally your urine should be a very pale yellow.)

For those who do endurance sports, or compete in the heat, it is also important to replace simple and complex sugars and electrolytes with a sports drink. There are a mind-boggling number of products to choose from. Research suggests that products that contain 6 to 8 percent mixed carbohydrates (E. Brown, no date) and electrolytes in the following mg/L ranges are most easily absorbed and utilized: sodium 400–1,100, chloride 500–1,500, potassium 120–225, calcium 45–225, and magnesium 10–100 (Brouns, Saris, and Schneider 1992).

Consuming sports drinks during endurance workouts lasting longer than ninety minutes, and during high-intensity workouts lasting longer than sixty minutes, maintains hydration and blood glucose, delivering fuel to working muscles, delaying fatigue, and improving end-of-workout or competition performance. Among nutritionally equivalent products, the best sports drink is not necessarily the one being hyped by your teammate or on some blog. Rather, it is the one you like enough to actually use—the one that tastes good and sits well in *your* system. Unless you are a sponsored athlete obligated to use a particular product, devote some time over the next month or so to finding a sports drink that tastes good and works well for you under competitive conditions.

Conditioning

For most sports, training is becoming increasingly scientific and deliberate. In addition to the topics covered previously, most highly competitive athletes devote time to developing strength, speed, endurance, flexibility, and core strength, along with other sport-specific skills. Hopefully your coach or trainer has already given you a basic set of strengthening and stretching routines. There are two benefits to doing these basic conditioning routines mindfully. First, tuning in to and being fully present with your body will allow you to get the most out of the physical exercises, and, second, doing so will simultaneously strengthen your mindfulness practice.

Travel, Time Zones, and Competing at Altitude

If you compete as a member of a team, your travel may often, if not always, be determined by your coach or team manager. If you compete as an individual, you may have more flexibility in your travel schedule. Either way, it is wise to develop travel routines that allow you to arrive physically, mentally, and emotionally ready to compete at your best. Small things can make a big difference:

- Writing, refining, and actually using a detailed packing list

- Arriving at the designated meeting place well before departure

- Having healthy food and plenty of decaffeinated fluids to drink (travel, particularly flying, is dehydrating)

- Using a bit of your travel time to do a mindfulness practice

- Having inspirational tunes, movies, or reading material available

- Being realistic about whether you will be able to sleep in the car, on the bus, or on the plane

- Chilling with your teammates

- Realizing that travel will take something out of you

- Planning an easier workout, or a longer, more gradual warm-up, to work out the kinks

- If you get to determine your own schedule, knowing whether you function best if you have maximum time at home, where you can maintain your routine and sleep in your own bed, or if you do best arriving early and having time to settle in and adapt to the venue

One last note, depending on the duration and nature of the event: most athletes benefit from setting their body clocks to local time and acclimating when competing at altitude. The longer the event (road cycling, marathon, triathlon, ultradistance race), the more important acclimation becomes. If possible:

- Allow at least one day of precompetition adjustment for each time zone crossed

- Adjust training loads and training times before departure

- Choose an evening flight when traveling east

- Switch clocks to the destination time zone before the flight departs

- Eat according to the destination time

- Hydrate and use earplugs, eye shades, melatonin, or light devices

- Shift training schedules upon arrival (Fatigue Science 2015)

- Get out into the sunshine to allow your body clock to adjust

- Add two weeks to your stay at the competition site to adapt to altitudes up to 2,300 meters and an additional week for each 610-meter increase (McArdle, Katch, and Katch 2007)

Periodization

There was a time not so long ago when highly successful athletes smoked, caroused, and then threw on their gear to compete at the highest level. Now most, but certainly not all, highly competitive athletes schedule their training on a yearlong cycle—conditioning in the preseason and aiming to peak for a handful of major competitions during the season. Endurance athletes, in particular, often chart out two to three peaks per season, designating specific cycles of increasing training intensity, tapering, competition, and recovery. Because it is physically impossible to remain peaked for an entire season, designating these specific periods, a process called *periodization*, will allow you to be at your best for your target competitions, be it your local 10K or century ride, nationals, worlds, or the Olympics.

Perhaps you are working with a coach who determines your schedule. If this is the case, hopefully she or he has already planned preseason conditioning, periods of skill development and increasing physical intensity, and competition, as well as times of consolidation, integration, restoration, and recovery. Even so, it can be helpful to bring some kind and curious attention to your annual schedule. Enter the following information on the very simple calendar below:

- The dates of your three to four target competitions

- The dates of your preseason

- The dates of your off-season

- The dates of any vacations, family events, significant school or work obligations such as finals or big projects, and special occasions that will affect your training

- Your "build" periods of increased training load

- Your taper periods (After a block of intense training, a taper is necessary to allow the body to recuperate and assimilate the efforts. It's important to clarify that tapering isn't a complete lack of training, or just really easy training. Rather, it entails specific reductions in the frequency, volume, and duration of your efforts, while maintaining some intensity.)

- Your rest-and-recovery periods (As with tapers, these are not periods of no training, but lighter training and fun cross-training.)

In combination, these precise adjustments of chronic-training load allow the body to maintain and maximize the benefits from the previous build cycle.

PERIODIZATION—YEARLY

	Week 1	Week 2	Week 3	Week 4
January				
February				
March				
April				
May				
June				
July				
August				
September				
October				
November				
December				

Now you have an outline of your annual calendar. At the beginning of each month you can create a more detailed weekly schedule using similar principles of days of intensity (builds) and days of recovery. In the future, you may want to start your annual calendar when your off-season begins.

Many athletes seriously underestimate the value of tapering, rest, and recovery, and they often overtrain prior to target competitions. Unfortunately, the result is that they end up depleted and burned out, sometimes with severe, medically diagnosed adrenal insufficiency and chronic fatigue.

After missing forty-six consecutive PGA cuts, Chip Beck, a champion golfer, acknowledged that he was burned out from the intensity of tournament play and that he should have taken a three to six-month break prior to burning out. He noted that "proper rest is essential for high-level performance" (Afremow 2013, 234). Perhaps if he had built tapers, rest, and recovery into his schedule at the beginning of his season he wouldn't have needed an unplanned, extended break. "You can't push, push, push all the time. You need to be rested and ready. It's like the rest in music is sometimes more important than the music itself" (Afremow 2013, 234).

Basic Concept: Wise Effort and Injury Prevention

In this section and the next we expand on the themes of work, rest, pushing through, and backing off that were introduced in the previous section. Together, micro moment-to-moment choices and macro big-picture choices will help you simultaneously surpass and honor your current limits and ultimately optimize your performance. Our general culture, and athletic culture in particular, tends to embrace the motto "No pain, no gain." And while it is true that in sports we must push beyond our limits to progress, it is also true that pushing too hard and too often can result in injury and physical, mental, or emotional burnout.

As the images on the next page demonstrate, there is a fine line between slacking off and pushing too hard. With mindfulness, you can discover the sweet spot, the middle path, the place where you are challenging yourself and improving without risking avoidable injury or burnout. This requires *listening* to the body, rather than the mind; the mind tends to under- or overestimate our abilities, saying things like *I'm done, I'll just skip this set,* or *I got this. It is not that bad. Just one more sequence.* Carli Lloyd, two-time Olympic gold medalist, 2015 World Cup champion, and 2015 and 2016 FIFA player of the year, notes that the experience of being injured was "a timely reminder of the importance of taking care of your body. The strength and vitality of your body are where it all starts. You need to listen to it and let it heal when it needs to heal" (Lloyd and Coffey 2016, 82).

Fatigue, aches, pains, and even injury are part of an athletic life, and there are definitely times when you should suck it up and play through the pain. However, as athletes, coaches,

THE DISTANCE
BETWEEN
WINNING &
LOSING

THE DISTANCE
BETWEEN
TRAINING &
INJURY

and a culture, we often take this mind-set to unhealthy extremes. If you are mindful, you can learn to notice the *early* physical signs of impending injury, as well as the physical—and often mental and emotional—signs of overtraining. Paying attention in this way will allow you to back off rather than push through and go over the edge.

Basic Concept: Energetic Bank Account

At any given moment we each have a specific amount of energy in our "energetic bank account." As an athlete, it is crucial that you generally maintain a substantial positive balance in your account. Three simple questions will allow you to track your energetic balance over time and make the moment-to-moment choices to maintain the positive balance that will support you in performing at your best:

1. What is the *current* balance in my energetic bank account?

2. Will this choice be a deposit to or a withdrawal from my energetic bank account?

3. What choices do I need to make to maintain a positive balance in my energetic bank account?

Obvious examples of athletes consciously choosing to maintain a positive energetic balance include Olympians who choose not to participate in the opening ceremonies because they are scheduled to compete in the first few days following the opening ceremonies, and Olympians who choose to both skip the opening ceremonies and not move into the Olympic Village until just before or after their events because they are scheduled to compete late in the games. Based on what they have learned—through years of competition—about maintaining a positive energetic balance, these athletes make the wisest choices possible in order to optimize their performance. And they make these choices knowing that regardless of the outcome of their Olympics, they will still be able to enjoy the closing ceremonies.

Activity: Maintaining a Positive Balance in Your Energetic Bank Account

To develop your ability to apply the principle of the energetic bank account in real time, begin by using the detailed "daily energetic bank balance" worksheet. Start by entering your current balance: on a scale of -10 (exhausted) to +10 (very energetic), how would you rate your current energy? This is your starting balance. Now enter your deposits (+1) and withdrawals (-1). Examples of deposits include a good night's sleep, a healthy meal, listening to music, hanging out with good friends, a good stretch and roll out, a bath, watching your favorite show or inspiring videos, relaxing with your pet, a recovery workout, a massage, an early date night, and resting in the Still Quiet Place. Examples of withdrawals include an intense workout; getting sick; a major project, test, or final exam; an argument with a family member, friend, teammate, or coach; breaking up with your boyfriend or girlfriend; and a major change or illness in your family or on your team.

By bringing your kind and curious attention to how you respond to certain circumstances you will learn *your personal value* for various deposits and withdrawals. For example, you might think an evening out with friends will be a deposit, only to discover the burgers left you feeling heavy and bloated, the time on your feet playing foosball and dancing tired your legs, and the soda kept you awake. This is not to say that you shouldn't go out with your friends, simply that you need to be aware of what it costs you so you can choose wisely when you want to make this type of withdrawal, and so you can make timely deposits to reestablish a positive balance. This is particularly important during an intense training block or before a target event.

Paying attention to these elements of health and preparation will make you less likely to suffer from burnout, overuse injuries, overtraining, adrenal insufficiency, and chronic fatigue syndrome. Ultimately, these practices will support you in finding flow in sports and in life. Ideally, over time you will be able to calculate a simplified weekly energetic bank balance, or simply track your balance by tuning in to your body and mentally noting deposits and withdrawals. However, if you are prone to overtraining, you may benefit from calculating your daily energetic bank balance for an extended period of time, until you internalize the process.

DAILY ENERGETIC BANK BALANCE

	Deposits	Withdrawals	Balance
Starting			
Sleep	+	−	=
Nutrition	+	−	=
Hydration	+	−	=
Training	+	−	=
Travel	+	−	=
Illness/injury	+	−	=
School	+	−	=
Work	+	−	=
Relationships	+	−	=
Fun	+	−	=
Other	+	−	=
Ending			

WEEKLY ENERGETIC BANK BALANCE

	Deposits	Withdrawals	Balance
Starting			
Monday	+	−	=
Tuesday	+	−	=
Wednesday	+	−	=
Thursday	+	−	=
Friday	+	−	=
Saturday	+	−	=
Sunday	+	−	=
Ending			

Activity: Precompetition Ritual

Many athletes find it helpful to create a precompetition ritual. Athletes create these rituals to bring their attention into the present moment, to lighten up, and to prepare their bodies, minds, and hearts for competition. Well-known examples of precompetition rituals include hurdler Michelle Jenneke dancing joyfully, Usain Bolt pointing to the sky before stepping into the starting blocks, and Michael Phelps blasting Eminem in the ready room. Stephen Curry, the 2015 and 2016 NBA MVP, has a playful, powerful, and extremely *mindful* pregame ritual. He has a tattoo of matching arrows pointing at each other, and before tip off he shows them to his wife. It "signifies the past is behind us and the future is in front of us, so we stay in the middle, in the moment. I smack my tattoo and she does the same" (Shipnuck 2016). Clearly, Curry feels that being present in the moment is so important he had a reminder tattooed on his body.

Research indicates that athletes who use preperformance routines are better able to overcome adversity and distraction. When male high school basketball players were asked to shoot free throws with and without their usual preshot routine, twenty out of twenty-five had lower scores during the no-routine condition (Gooding and Gardner 2009).

If you already have a precompetition ritual, write it down in detail here. If not, make up something *simple* that you feel will work well for you. Ideally, because sometimes *s--t happens*, your ritual should be simple, flexible, and as snafu free as possible. Include one playful element that has you smile and helps you lighten up.

1. _____

2. _____

3. _____

4. _____

Whether you have a tried-and-true ritual or are creating one for the first time, bring kind and curious attention to each element of your ritual. You can simplify, tweak, and refine your ritual whenever you want. Consider the following:

- Does your ritual bring you into the moment?

- Does your ritual help you tune in to your body?

- Does your ritual support you in watching thoughts (chapter 5) and befriending feelings (chapter 6)?

- Is there any part of your ritual that you want to switch up? To keep it fresh? To support you as you develop a new physical, mental, or emotional skill?

- Does your ritual have an element of fun or joy?

- At the end of your ritual how do your body, mind, and heart feel?

Giving Yourself the Gift of Mindfulness

Throughout your competitive career you will want to continue to devote time to refining each aspect of your physical preparation. During the next competitive cycle bring your kind and curious attention to refining one or two elements of health and preparation that influence your performance. Perhaps there are areas where you feel sure that you know what works best for you, and others you feel you could tweak. Maybe there are things you want to read up on or speak to your coach, trainer, or nutritionist about. Use each training and competition cycle to learn what works well for you and what doesn't. Realize that things change over time and that sometimes, despite your best efforts, things don't go as planned and you will need to adapt. And if in this moment paying attention to all these elements of preparation feels overwhelming (an energetic withdrawal), keep it simple; remember, in the end the crucial element is maintaining a positive balance in your energetic bank account.

CHAPTER 5

Getting Your Head in the Game

Thinking too much takes me out of my game and I forget what to do with my body.

—Julia Mancuso, 2014 Olympic bronze medalist in
women's super combined downhill skiing

All too often as athletes we are distracted by random thoughts—the argument we just had with our best friend or our roommate, a history final, a work deadline, the last play, the score, a teammate's comment, a parent's outburst, or a coach's disappointed shake of the head. Now that you have learned to rest your attention in the Still Quiet Place, you can begin to notice when *and* where your mind wanders. When you become aware that your attention has wandered, during mindfulness practice or during athletic training or competition, you can return to the present moment by bringing your kind and curious attention to the breath, the physical sensations in your body, or the sights and sounds of the competitive arena.

Basic Concept: Thought Watching

In his book *Open*, Andre Agassi offers an honest example of mind-wandering during competition. He describes playing Boris Becker in the semifinals at Wimbledon in 1995:

> I feel something snap. Not my hip—my mind. I'm suddenly unable to control my thoughts. I'm thinking of Pete [Sampras], waiting. I'm thinking of my sister Rita, whose husband, Pancho, just lost a long bout with stomach cancer. I'm thinking of Becker… I'm thinking of Brooke… All these thoughts go crashing through my mind, making me feel scattered, fractured, and this allows Becker to capture the momentum. He never gives it back. He wins in four sets. (2009, 208)

Over time, with mindfulness you can learn to use natural pauses in play to refocus your attention. For example, many tennis players use the moments before the serve to breathe, bounce the ball, and bring their attention fully into the present moment—the physical sensations, rhythms, and sounds of bouncing and catching the ball. Soccer players use throw-ins, penalty kicks, and kickoffs to briefly pause, breathe, check in with themselves, and scan the field to note the positions of their teammates and opponents, thus bringing their complete attention to the here and now. Phil Jackson, champion NBA basketball player and coach, understood the importance of focusing on the present moment:

> But what the players really needed was a way to quiet the chatter in their minds and focus on the business of winning basketball games… [Mindfulness] is an easily accessible technique for quieting the restless mind and focusing attention on whatever is happening in the present moment. This is extremely useful for basketball players, who often have to make split-second decisions under enormous pressure. (2014, 17–18)

Practice: Thought Watching

In this practice, you will learn how to watch your thoughts. You can download an audio recording of the following practice at http://www.newharbinger.com/40217.

> While it is useful to notice when we are lost in thought and return our attention to the here and now, it can also be useful to bring our kind and curious attention to our habits of thinking. One of my favorites ways to do this is to simply rest in the Still Quiet Place and then watch thoughts pass by, like watching a parade.
>
> With practice you can notice that thoughts come and go, that some thoughts are small and shy, while others are loud and colorful.
>
> Begin by resting in stillness and quietness, and then, when you are ready, gently bringing your kind and curious attention to watching the parade of thoughts march by. Whenever you notice that you are marching in the parade, lost in thought, return to standing on the sidewalk by returning your attention to the breath. Then, when you are safely on the sidewalk, and your attention is stable, you can begin watching the thoughts again.

Practice: Bubbles

Another way to play with thought watching is to blow bubbles. If you are doubtful, it may help you to know that I have shared this practice with many athletes, including hardcore high school offensive lineman, and they found it useful. So, if you want to give it a try, buy a container of bubbles. Open it and simply blow bubbles in silence for a few moments. Or, if you don't have any bubbles, you simply imagine that you are blowing bubbles. Then ask yourself the following questions:

What happens with the bubbles?

They float, they settle, they pop.

Do they all pop?

Eventually.

Are they the same size?

No, some are smaller, some are bigger.

Do they move at the same speed?

No, some are faster, some are slower.

Are bubbles like anything that happens in our minds? (Here's a hint: What do you call the thing above a cartoon character's head?)

Yes. It's a thought bubble.

How are thoughts and bubbles similar?

Do all your thoughts eventually pop and disappear?

Do you occasionally have clumps of thoughts?

Using the analogies of watching a parade or watching bubbles, you may begin to notice patterns in your thinking, and how thinking is associated with emotions and physical sensations. It can be particularly helpful to watch your thoughts before a big competition, or after a tough practice, significant loss, or major win (especially because you may get cocky). Bobby Jones said, "Competitive sports are played mainly on a five-and-a-half inch court, the space between your ears." His understanding of this mind-performance connection may help explain why he was the most successful amateur golfer ever, frequently beating the pros. Here are more questions you can ask yourself as you practice Thought Watching:

What are your thoughts about practice or the game?

How do you *think* you played?

How do you *think* the team played?

What are your thoughts about the upcoming competition?

Can you remember that you don't need to believe these thoughts, take them personally, or act on them?

And now can you let these thoughts go? And bring your attention to this moment, your breath, the chill in the air, the setting sun?

The following discussion that occurred after a thought watching practice with a group of fifth-grade basketball players may help you understand the usefulness of this practice for athletes of all ages and skill levels.

One morning, while doing a thought watching practice in a class where the majority of the boys had been rather skeptical of mindfulness, the boys noticed that many of their thoughts were about the basketball game they'd be playing that afternoon. They had lost the previous game, and now they were up against a team they *thought* was better than they were. Many of them were worried about losing, playing poorly, and letting their teammates down. They wanted to win.

During our previous sessions, one boy in particular had consistently put effort into being "cool," "funny" (that is, "disrespectful"), and less than participatory in the way that some fifth-grade boys can be. I asked him, "If you're thinking about winning and losing, and the outcome of the game, is your head *really* in the game? Is it really in what's happening right here, right now?" His eyes got big. His mouth hung open. He was "in"; mindfulness was now relevant to him. It helped to be able to tell the class that two of the most successful teams in the history of professional basketball, the Los Angeles Lakers and the Chicago Bulls, used mindfulness skills to bring their attention to actually playing the game—to the ball, the hoop, their teammates, and their opponents.

Activity: Nine Dots

Now that you have a feel for thought watching, you can apply this skill to working on a puzzle. First, take a moment to breathe and rest in stillness and quietness.

When you're ready, give yourself five minutes to try to solve this puzzle. As you're trying to solve the puzzle, notice the thoughts that come and go, and notice how you talk to yourself.

NINE DOTS

Below is an arrangement of nine dots. Connect all the dots by drawing four straight lines without lifting your pencil from the paper, and without retracing any line. The lines may cross.

●   ●   ●

●   ●   ●

●   ●   ●

Before you look at the solution (in the appendix), take some time to write about your experience. What did you say to yourself as you tried to solve the puzzle? There is no right or wrong response to this question. Just be real with yourself.

_____

_____

_____

Here are some things that other athletes have said out loud, or silently to themselves, while trying to solve this puzzle: "Puzzles are dumb." "I can't get this." "I'll figure it out." "I suck at math and puzzles." "I got it!" "I'll just google it." "What does this have to do with baseball?" "I love these kinds of games." "I'm stupid." "I give up."

Now that you know what others have said, is there anything you might add to what you wrote before? Recall what it was like trying to do the puzzle, and then take a moment to write down three more things you said to yourself. Again, there's no right or wrong response here. And remember, it is very helpful to be aware of your patterns and habits of thinking.

_____

_____

_____

Now take a look at what you wrote and answer the following questions by circling the most accurate answer.

Do you often say similar things to yourself when facing other
challenges, such as doing a difficult homework assignment,
taking a test, working on a challenging project,
or learning a new athletic skill?   Yes.   No.   Sometimes.

Was what you said to yourself mostly kind or unkind?

Was it mostly helpful or discouraging?

Was it mostly true or untrue?

When you try something new and challenging, what are you generally tempted to do?

Quit.   Keep trying.   Cheat.   Ask for help.   Other: _____

What could you have said to yourself that would have been more kind and helpful?

_____

_____

If you solved the puzzle ("won"), what thoughts and feelings came with this experience? If you haven't solved the puzzle, here are a couple of hints: There are actually multiple solutions. The most common ones start in each corner, and all of the solutions involve thinking outside the box. Give yourself another five minutes to play with the puzzle. See if you can be kind and encouraging with yourself. If you've already given up or are unable to encourage yourself, do your best to bring kindness and curiosity to the experiences of giving up and being unkind just as they are, in this moment.

Okay, enough! The solution is in the appendix, and before you turn to look, please know that this exercise isn't about getting the right answer; it's about bringing your kind and curious attention (yes, this phrase will be repeated over and over until it's lodged in your head and your heart) to your life. So when you see the solution to the puzzle, do your best to simply notice your thoughts and feelings with kindness and curiosity.

Reflection: Thinking Outside the Box

The solutions to the Nine Dots puzzle required thinking outside the box. With kindness and curiosity, consider some of the boxes (categories) that you put yourself in, and that others put you in.

What kinds of boxes do you put yourself in? Some common boxes are thoughts like *I am terrible at penalty kicks. I am clutch at free throws. I suck at math. I am a starter. I'll always be a bench player. I am too small to play solid D.*

Write down three boxes that describe how you think of yourself.

_____

_____

_____

Now consider whether these boxes feel helpful, true, or big enough. Are any of the boxes a source of stress? Circle one: Yes.   No.   Sort of.

Many of the boxes we put ourselves in can create stress. It is easy to see how negative or unkind boxes, such as *I am terrible at penalty kicks*, create stress. It can be more difficult to see how the positive boxes create stress, and they definitely can. If one of your boxes is *I'm a starter*, then what happens when you don't start?

Boxes can be helpful and serve a function, and they never tell the whole story. If you have a history of "choking" in big moments, you can acknowledge the *past*, and in this new, now moment develop new skills. The past choking isn't permanent—it isn't who you are; it doesn't define you. You are (we all are) so much more than your boxes. So it is helpful to be aware of our boxes, and at the same time we shouldn't take them too seriously or let them define us.

Perhaps one of the most inspiring stories of an athlete not letting other people's thought bubbles and limiting boxes define him is that of Stephen Curry. During his career, Curry has popped many thought bubbles and stepped outside numerous boxes—*not tall enough, not athletic enough, scrawny, played for Davidson, at best a sixth man, chronic ankle injuries, multiple surgeries, fourth-quarter turnovers, should be traded for Chris Paul*—to become the 2015 and 2016 NBA MVP (M. Thompson 2015).

Activity: A Challenge

Here's a new and challenging drill… What thoughts and feelings appear as you read the words "Here's a new and challenging drill?" Do you have a sense of *Let's do this*, or *Ugh, I'm not in the mood?* Are you curious? Excited? Nervous? Simply notice whatever thoughts and feelings show up without judging them as good or bad, or right or wrong.

Okay, now here's the challenge. Get five large paper clips and your cell phone or a stopwatch. Separate the paper clips and set them on the table. Before you begin, take ten slow deep breaths. Then, time yourself, and using *only* your dominant hand, the hand you write with, link all five paper clips together end to end in a chain. Before you begin, there is one additional part to the exercise. While you are connecting your paper clips, do your best to notice your thinking. Most elite athletes can do this task in thirty seconds.

What did you say to yourself, either internally or out loud?

_____

_____

Were your thoughts kind or unkind? Helpful or unhelpful?

Do you have thoughts like these when you are training and competing? When you are doing homework, taking a test, working on a project, or talking to someone you are interested in?

Basic Concept: Unkind Mind

If some, or a lot, of your internal dialogue is unkind, unhelpful, and untrue, please know you are not alone. Most people have this type of negative internal chatter and self-critical play-by-play; I fondly call it Unkind Mind. As author Grace Lichtenstein writes, Unkind Mind is our real opponent: "Your opponent, in the end, is never really the player on the other side of the net, or the swimmer in the next lane, or the team on the other side of the field, or even the bar you must high-jump. Your opponent is yourself, your negative internal voices."

Sports psychologist Keith Kaufman has conducted multiple research studies regarding the benefits of mindfulness in sports. His research supports a primary premise of this book, that with practice you can learn to watch Unkind Mind without believing it, taking it personally, or letting it prevent you from fully expressing your talent.

> Athletes can learn to recognize their mind wandering toward thoughts about limitations during competition (e.g., "I can't sustain this pace") but then mindfully label these experiences as just thoughts, let them go and bring attention back to a present moment anchor like their breathing. Through this process, athletes can free themselves from judgments that might unnecessarily determine their limits. (Kaufman, Glass, and Pineau 2016, 160)

In your own words, describe how the practice of simply noticing your thoughts without believing them or taking them personally can be helpful during training and competition.

_____

_____

_____

Activity: Comparison

Now, what if I told you that most elite athletes connect the papers clips in three minutes rather than thirty seconds?

What thoughts arise?

_____

_____

_____

In training and competition, when you compare yourself to others, what patterns of thinking and feeling arise?

_____

_____

_____

Do you feel that these habits of thinking and feeling help you perform at your best? If so, how?

_____

_____

_____

If not, why?

_____

_____

_____

As the paper clip exercise and your answers to the questions above show, our performance can be affected when we compare ourselves to others. George Mumford, mindfulness coach for the Chicago Bulls, Los Angeles Lakers, New York Knicks, and other elite athletes, writes that he's seen plenty of athletes "who had talent that was out of this world, but they didn't believe it. As a result they would withdraw, close down, and never fully express that talent simply because their self-critic had a vice grip on their minds" (2015, 178). We will explore the habit of comparison again in chapter 9, "Mistakes, Self-Compassion, and Intentions."

Note to Coaches

The paper clip activity can be done in teams. Divide your athletes into two or more teams. Have each team stand in a line, shoulder to shoulder. Instruct all of the athletes in each line to put their paper clips in their nondominant hands. Then explain that the teams will be racing each other to link the paper clips end to end in a long chain, using only the athletes' nondominant hands. To begin, the first and second athlete in each line will link their paper clips using only their nondominant hands. Once the first two papers clips are linked end to end, the second athlete will turn to the third athlete to link paper clips, and so on, until in sequence all of the athletes in the line have linked paper clips and the team's end-to-end paper clip chain is complete. This activity tends to elicit the types of thinking and comments that teammates direct toward themselves and each other during training and competition.

Activity: Positive Scanning and the Magic Ratio

Most human beings, and particularly athletes committed to improving performance, habitually engage in negative scanning. We routinely look for and assess what we "did wrong" and what we could do "better" in practice, competition, and life. While there is value in this type of reflection, many highly competitive athletes take this to a potentially self-defeating extreme.

So it can be helpful to balance the habit of negative scanning with *positive scanning*—that is, looking for and acknowledging things you did well. Research shows that personal and business relationships function optimally when the ratio of positive to negative interactions is at least five to one (Gottman 1994; Losada 1999; Losada and Heaphy 2004); this is the magic ratio. Do your best to maintain this ratio in *your relationship with yourself*. After each practice or competition, acknowledge and appreciate at least five specific things you did well.

Use the worksheet on the following page to establish the habit of positive scanning. Truly appreciate your effort, your support of your teammates, your willingness to follow specific coaching, and your refining of a particular skill or technique. And for this exercise make the *choice* to simply ignore Unkind Mind's usual *Yes, but* thinking and negative scanning.

POSITIVE SCANNING: WHAT I DID WELL

Monday

1. _____
2. _____
3. _____
4. _____
5. _____

Tuesday

1. _____
2. _____
3. _____
4. _____
5. _____

Wednesday

1. _____
2. _____
3. _____
4. _____
5. _____

Thursday

1. _____
2. _____

3. _____

4. _____

5. _____

Friday

1. _____

2. _____

3. _____

4. _____

5. _____

Saturday

1. _____

2. _____

3. _____

4. _____

5. _____

Sunday

1. _____

2. _____

3. _____

4. _____

5. _____

Activity: Positive Inner Instruction

In *The Inner Game of Tennis*, Tim Gallwey writes, "'You rolled your racket over again,' can be said as a biting self-criticism or a simple observation of fact, depending on the tone of voice. The imperatives, 'Watch the ball,' or 'Move your feet,' can be uttered as an encouragement to the body or as a belittling condemnation of its past performance" (2008, 17). This biting self-criticism and belittling condemnation that Gallwey describes exemplifies the harsh inner dialogue of Unkind Mind. List five things Unkind Mind frequently says to you. If nothing comes to mind right now, that's fine—enjoy it. And if some sayings come to mind, jot them down so that when you hear them you will know they are just Unkind Mind talking, and you don't need to believe them or take them seriously.

1. _____

2. _____

3. _____

4. _____

5. _____

On the next page are some common Unkind Mind sayings.

YOU IDIOT. I'll never get this.

HE IS BETTER.   **I am weak.**

Again?!   WE'RE GOING TO LOSE.

I AM FAT.   I MESSED UP AGAIN.

I'm hopeless.   F--K!   I aM SLOW.

I suck.   I ALWAYS CHOKE.

I'LL always BE a BENCHWARMER.

Now list five helpful things you can say to yourself when you are struggling. This is the practice of positive inner instruction. If you are unsure of what to write, consider what you say to a friend or teammate who is having a rough day, or what a supportive friend or teammate says to you when you're off your game.

1. _____

2. _____

3. _____

4. _____

5. _____

Below are some common Kind Mind sayings.

YOU GOT THIS.

Easy, dude.

Sweet.

GIVE IT ANOTHER TRY.

Nice shot.

BETTER.

GREAT D.

Take a deep breath.

THAT'S IT.

You go, girl!

JUST LIKE IN PRACTICE.

Beautiful!

YOU'RE DOING JUST GREAT.

You'll get the next one.

Basic Concept: Beyond Unkind Mind— Nonjudgmental Awareness

Positive scanning is a beneficial counterbalance to the relentless critical chatter of Unkind Mind. Yet, ultimately, the real antidote for Unkind Mind—and an essential element of finding flow—is kindness and curiosity, also known as *nonjudgmental awareness*—simply observing your performance without judging it as good or bad, right or wrong, better or worse. You have already practiced this type of kind and curious awareness with the Body Scan (chapter 3), Stretch and Balance (downloadable audio recording available at http://www.newharbinger .com/40217), and Thought Watching (chapter 5) practices. This clear, open observation will allow you to sense the natural adjustments and intuitive physical tweaks that will optimize your performance. And, it bypasses common disadvantageous mental habits: overthinking, analyzing, comparing, critiquing, and trying too hard. As Jim Afremow, author of *The Champion's Mind*, explains, critical

> inner commentary keeps you one step removed from the actual performance, rather than fully focused on the performance. Always be athletic on the field of play. Do not take on the additional role of being your own coach, parent, spectator, or shrink. Stay in athlete mode by focusing all of your energy on execution, not self-analysis. (2013, 77)

If you are unsure of how to access this nonjudgmental awareness, begin with kindness and curiosity. Ask yourself openhearted questions. The following excerpt from Tim Gallwey's *The Inner Game of Tennis* offers specific examples of kind and curious questions a tennis player might ask about a forehand shot:

> How is your weight distributed during preparation and at impact? What happens to your balance during the shot?… What kinds of sounds do your feet make on the court as you move? When the ball approaches you, do you retreat, advance or hold your ground? (2008, 62)

One kind and curious question is enough! Asking multiple questions will likely trigger excessive thinking. The beauty of one simple question is that it gets you out of your head and back into your body, and then your body can naturally make intuitive adjustments and corrections. As a player coached by Gallwey noted, "Instead of seeing what was wrong with my backhand, I just started observing, and improvement seemed to happen on its own" (Gallwey 2008, 24).

Giving Yourself the Gift of Mindfulness

Over the next week or so, do the following:

- Practice Thought Watching every day.

- Any time you realize you are lost in thought during practice and competition, return your attention to the present moment, to your breath, to the feel of your feet on the ground or the air on your skin.

- Be aware of Unkind Mind.

- Practice positive scanning and positive inner instruction.

- When you are stuck in your head, ask yourself one simple question about your body movement; this will bring you into your body and the moment.

CHAPTER 6

Befriending Feelings

The reality is that optimal competitive performance often occurs with strong and uncomfortable (sometimes incorrectly judged to be "negative") internal experiences, and any suggestion that optimal performance requires the absence of such experiences is simply wrong and flies in the face of the empirical [research] and anecdotal [personal] evidence.

—Zella Moore, sports psychologist and mindfulness researcher

In the last chapter you practiced bringing your kind and curious attention to the thoughts associated with training and competition. In this chapter you will practice doing the same with feelings or emotions. One well-known key to finding flow is developing the ability to "have your feelings without your feelings having you." What does this mean? To "have your feelings" means you're able to be aware of what you're feeling in the moment. "Without your feelings having you" means your feelings don't negatively affect your performance, control your behavior, or have you say or do something that you might regret.

Basic Concept: It's Okay to Feel Anxious

It is common to feel nervous before a competition, overjoyed after a big win, and heartbroken after serious loss. And with practice you can learn to rest in stillness and quietness and watch as these emotional waves ebb and flow. You can learn to recognize the rapid heart rate and jitteriness before competition as signs that your body is prepared and ready. You can enjoy the postwin high and accept the postloss low as the temporary experiences that they are.

This doesn't mean pretending you are calm or fine when you are not. Rather, the suggestion is that you hold the intense experiences of competition with kindness and curiosity, and learn to observe them from the vantage point of your still quiet essence. Mindfulness teacher Pema Chödrön invites us to explore this powerful way of relating to feelings:

The central question of a warrior's training is not how we avoid uncertainty and fear but how we relate to discomfort. How do we practice with difficulty, with our emotions, with the unpredictable encounters of an ordinary day? (2002, 7)

Most anxiety is due to worrying about the future, the fantasy or nightmare of how we imagine the practice, tryout, or competition will go. And most depression is related to the negative scanning of past events. So when you are overwhelmed by intense feelings, breathe, feel your feet on the ground, come back into the present moment, and simply allow the feelings to be, without trying to change them, fix them, or get rid of them.

Once, when I was offering an introductory session for youths and parents, a mom raised her hand and said, "I am an anxious person, and my kids are both anxious, we struggle with severe anxiety…" As she went on and on, everyone in the room began to feel more and more anxious. When she stopped, I simply said, "You know it is okay to *feel* anxious? Right?"

When I said this the anxious energy in the room evaporated. The woman and her children visibly softened and relaxed. They really *got* that it's okay to feel anxious, that they could accept their anxiety with kindness and curiosity. At some point in her life, she had been told or had decided that she and her kids *shouldn't* be anxious, and that they needed to do something, change something, or fix something. Ever since that moment she had felt anxious about feeling anxious. My question opened the possibility of simply resting in stillness and quietness, observing the anxiety, and letting it be, without resisting it or thinking something is wrong—that is, she realized she could have anxiety without anxiety having her.

Not only is it okay to feel anxious, but it is also okay to feel stressed, depressed, excited, jealous, overjoyed, and angry. Consider what Andrew Talansky, a professional cyclist who rode in the Tour de France, says about fear:

I came to embrace fear. You might not hear athletes say it often, but we are all afraid. If you're not, then odds are you're not pushing yourself to your limits. I've come to realize that fear will never leave. Fear of failure. Fear of not achieving my goals. Fear of giving all of yourself to something and still coming up short. That's probably my greatest fear.

What I came to realize is that those fears don't need to go away. They don't need to be blocked out. (2016)

Practice: Befriending Feelings

You can download an audio recording of this practice at http://www.newharbinger.com/40217.

This practice involves bringing kind and curious attention to your feelings, or emotions. As usual, sit or lie in a comfortable position…find the breath in your belly…and rest in stillness and quietness.… When you are ready, simply note whatever feelings are present. Sometimes it can be helpful to name the feeling or feelings. Some feelings may have ordinary names, like angry, happy, sad, or excited, and others may have more unusual names, like stormy, bubbly, fiery, or empty. It can be helpful to remember that feelings may be small and subtle, and kind of shy, or big and intense, that feelings may shift over time, and that there may be layers of feelings.

Once you've brought your kind and curious attention to a particular feeling, and you've named it, notice where the feeling lives in your body: sitting in your chest, moving in your belly, thrumming in your head.... Also notice how the emotion feels in your body. Does it feel small? Heavy? Hard? Warm? Jagged? Light? Soft? Smooth? Big? Cool? Is it moving or still?...

If any of these questions shifts you into thinking about the feeling rather than experiencing it, just breathe and return to being with the feeling.

Now, notice whether the feeling has a color, or colors, or imagine that it does—perhaps dark red, pale blue, or bright green.... And if it doesn't have a color, that is fine.

And listen to see whether the feeling has a sound, such as giggling, groaning, weeping, or whining.... And if there's no sound, no worries.

To end the practice, notice how you feel now, and congratulate yourself for taking the time to be with, and befriend, your feelings. Then, return your attention to the breath and rest in stillness and quietness for a bit longer.

Remember, you can rest in stillness and befriend your feelings whenever you want.

When you are ready, take three slow deep breaths in your own time.... Open your eyes and move into your next moment.

Reflection: How Did It Feel to Befriend Your Feelings?

Take some time now to reflect on your experience with the Befriending Feelings practice.

What feeling or feelings were present?

_____

Where did you *feel* these emotions in your body?

_____

How did the emotions *feel*—tight, fluid…?

_____

Did the emotions have any colors?

_____

Did they have any sounds?

_____

Activity: Having Your Feelings Without Your Feelings Having You

You just practiced befriending your feelings. There is real power in learning to have your feelings without your feelings having you. "In my view," writes Phil Jackson, champion NBA player and coach, "the key to becoming a successful NBA player is not learning the coolest highlight-reel moves. It's learning to control your emotions and keep your mind focused on the game…how to stay cool under pressure and maintain your equanimity after crushing losses or ecstatic wins" (2014, 281).

Can you think of a time in the recent past where your feelings had you? Describe the situation, how you felt, and what happened.

_____

_____

_____

_____

Looking back now, how might befriending your feelings have helped you in this situation?

_____

_____

_____

_____

Reflection: Dealing with Feelings

It can be helpful to understand that each of us tends to have habits, certain ways we usually deal with our feelings. Without mindfulness, most of us tend to live within a fairly narrow range on the continuum between ignoring (suppressing) feelings and being overwhelmed (controlled) by them. Take a moment and consider what you tend to do with intense feelings.

For those of us who usually ignore and suppress our feelings, the Befriending Feelings practice can help us bring kindness and curiosity to our emotions, making us more emotionally intelligent. For those of us who tend to be flooded and overwhelmed by our feelings, it can be helpful to take some time to really settle into the Still Quiet Place *before* doing the Befriending Feelings practice. With practice, we can all learn to have our feelings without our feelings having us (at least most of the time). Ultimately, this allows us to find flow and perform at our best.

During an interview a reporter tried to get a reaction out of MLB player Shawn Green, asking him why he didn't throw his helmet or engage in other emotional displays when he was playing poorly. Green's response embodies the idea of having your feelings without them having you:

> Where's the competitive advantage in my getting lost in my emotions? The best thing I can do to help my team is to take it one at-bat at a time. Anger and rage aren't going to help me get more hits. Being focused will help. That's all I can do. (2011, 131)

Basic Concept: Tuning Your Instrument

There is a well-known question: How often do you need to tune a violin before it stays tuned? If you know even a little bit about music, you know that a violinist tunes her violin before every rehearsal and performance. It is the same for athletes. Once we have deliberately brought our attention to our bodies, minds, and hearts and have a feel for our physical, mental, and emotional tone, we can gently tune ourselves—taking a few deep breaths to settle into stillness and quietness, doing a few quick bounces to reenergize and focus. Ideally these little adjustments are wise *responses* to how we are in the moment, rather than desperate *reactions* to circumstances. We will explore the distinction between responding and reacting in chapter 7. For now, I trust that you can feel the difference between "I am too nervous; I need to calm down right now" and "I am aware that I am anxious and I am going to take a few slow deep breaths and just watch the anxiety."

Basic Concept: Emotion Theory—Watching the Waves

In this section you will learn a bit about emotion theory—the science and the natural time course of emotions. In combination with the Befriending Feelings practice, an understanding of emotion theory will support you in becoming more aware of your emotions in real time, and in having your feelings without your feelings having you; ultimately, it will increase your ability to experience flow in training, competition, and life.

Psychologist Paul Ekman (2007) has studied emotional expression all over the world, from very developed countries to areas without Internet access or even TVs, and has developed a scientific framework of emotion that he calls emotion theory, which can support us in our efforts to be mindful of our emotions. So far, Dr. Ekman has found that there are seven universal emotions that all human beings share: happiness, fear, anger, sadness, surprise, contempt, and disgust. More importantly, and relevant to mindfulness, his work has revealed that each primary emotion has a very specific facial expression and body presentation, and that emotions have a natural time course. Take a moment now to make each of the following facial expressions. Notice how you *feel* as you try each one.

Open your eyes wide. Raise your eyebrows, drop your jaw, and open your mouth in an O shape. How do you feel when you make this facial expression? What do you notice in your body? What emotion does this express?

_____

_____

Using your facial muscles, curve the corners of your mouth down toward your shoulders. How do you feel? What do you notice in your body? What emotion does this express?

_____

_____

Again, using your cheeks and other facial muscles, gently curve the corners of your mouth up toward the outside corners of your eyes. How do you feel when you make this facial expression? What do you notice in your body? What emotion does this express?

_____

_____

What's fascinating is that even though you did simple, incomplete versions of the facial expressions that Dr. Ekman describes, you probably sensed the emotions in your body. For example, when making the facial expression for surprise, you may have felt a little surprised. When frowning, you may have felt slightly sad, and when smiling, you may have felt a bit happier. As with the previous Befriending Feelings practice and the embodying emotions activity later in the chapter, this exercise allows you to experience a basic truth: your emotions and your physical experience are very closely connected.

Another interesting thing about emotions is that when we don't suppress or magnify them, they tend to have their own natural time course or rhythm. In your daily life, can you notice when an emotion begins, peaks, and ends?

Ekman presents the natural time course of emotions as a—perhaps oversimplified—wave or bell curve. This representation demonstrates that just like the breath, emotions have a beginning, a middle (or peak, also called the refractory period), and an end.

Basic Concept: Refractory Period

Dr. Ekman uses the term *refractory period* to define the peak of an emotion.

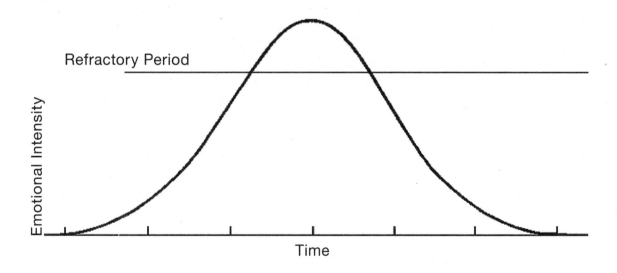

During the refractory period, emotion takes over and we can't think clearly. In these moments, we're controlled by an older part of the brain sometimes called the lizard brain or reptilian brain. When this happens, we're in fight, flight, or freeze mode. This means that, like lizards, we can only fight, run away, or freeze. We aren't able to use our full human minds and hearts to choose our behavior, to respond rather than react, to get back in the game.

Take a few minutes to describe a time when you were in the refractory period.

_____

_____

_____

Fortunately, mindfulness can help us notice the beginning of an emotion, the refractory period, and the end of the emotion. When we're *aware* that we're in the grips of an emotion, stuck in the refractory period, we can only make very *basic* choices—at least some of the time—holding our tongue, walking away, or simply continuing to play.

Activity: Watching Your Emotional Waves

I like to use the analogy of watching waves when describing how mindfulness can help us deal with intense emotions. Often, strong emotions take us by surprise, like a rogue wave. Mindfulness is our early-warning system. If we're paying attention, we can see the very first ripples of an emotion. When we notice an emotional wave building, getting bigger and more powerful, we can choose to move to higher ground so the wave doesn't come crashing down on us. George Mumford, mindfulness coach for the Chicago Bulls, Los Angeles Lakers, New York Knicks, and other elite athletes, writes that mindfulness

> helps us…to truly understand that whatever waves are rocking our personal boats—or whatever stresses or challenges are flying our way in the practice of our sport—we have a choice to reconnect to that deep place within [the Still Quiet Place] at all times and to act from that place between stimulus and response [that is, to choose our behavior]. (2015, 80)

While our emotional waves may vary from day to day, we all tend to have emotional patterns. It may help you to know that, in truth, most of our emotional time lines are not as smooth as Dr. Ekman's curve above. When I have asked athletes to draw their emotional diagrams for anger, they have bravely and honestly drawn images like these:

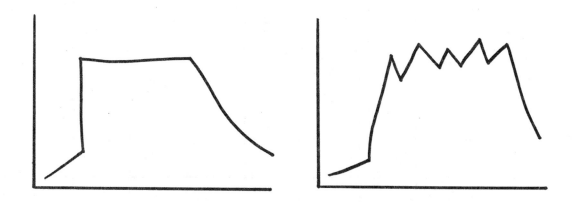

Recall times when you experienced the following basic emotions, and then draw your pattern for each emotion using the grids.

Anger

Time

Happiness

Time

Sadness

Time

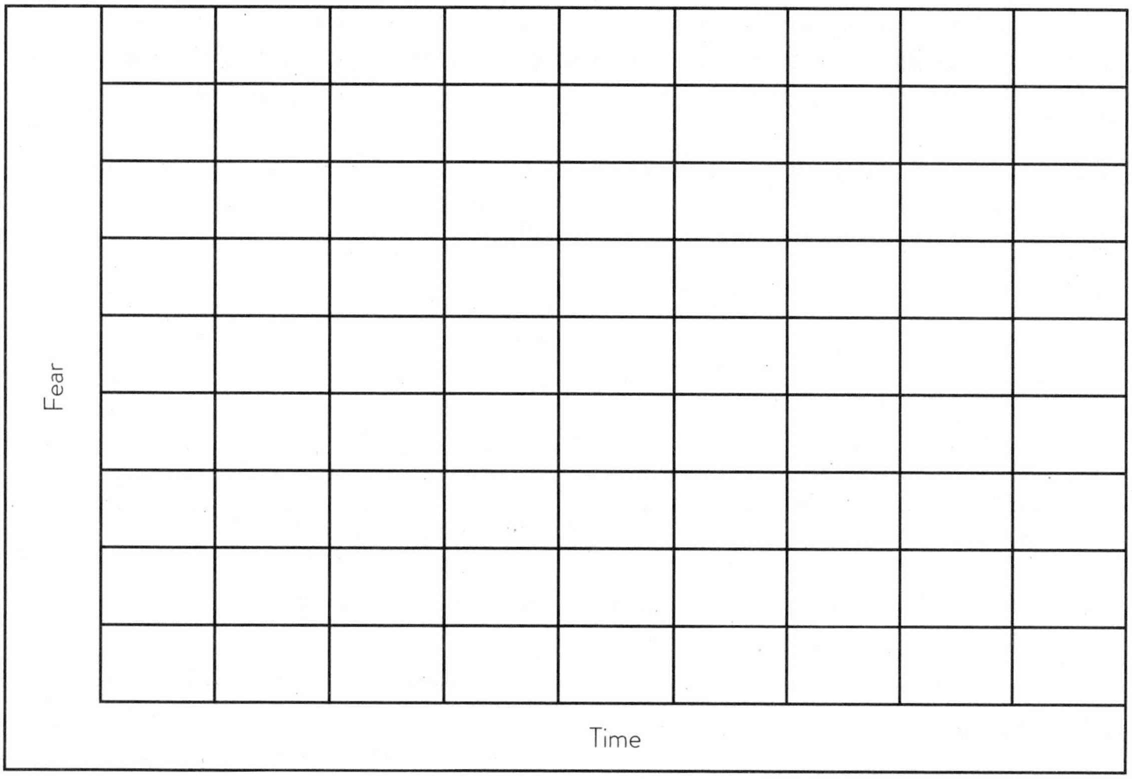

<!-- Graph: vertical axis labeled "Fear", horizontal axis labeled "Time", blank grid -->

Fear

Time

Activity: Embodying Emotion

Knowing your general emotional patterns can be very useful. This knowledge allows you to recognize emotions early and either move to higher ground or ride out the emotional wave before you act. A key element to being aware of emotional waves is recognizing *how* different emotions *feel* in your body. Acting out some basic emotions will help you get a feel for this. Even if you are reluctant or want to blow off this exercise, please give it a try. Find a private space, maybe a bathroom, your bedroom, or a corner of your yard, where you can do this exercise in peace. Because anger is very common and often problematic, you may want to begin with it.

Take a moment to rest in stillness, then take one step forward and show a small amount of anger—say, 25 percent—with your body and face. Feel what 25-percent anger feels like in your body, mind, and heart.

Now step back and rest in stillness. When you're ready, step forward again and show a medium amount of anger—say, 50 percent—with your body and face. Feel what this feels like in your body, mind, and heart.

Now step back and rest in stillness. When you're ready, step forward again and show a large amount of anger—say 75 percent—with your body and face. If you feel inspired, you can even add a sound or a motion. Feel what this feels like in your body, mind, and heart.

What happens in your body when you show anger? Describe, in detail, how your legs, arms, hands, chest, and face feel.

_____

_____

_____

_____

What thoughts did you notice when you acted angry, or *embodied* anger?

_____

_____

_____

Is anger familiar? Circle one: Yes.   No.   Sort of.

How often do you feel angry? Circle one: Often.   Sometimes.   Rarely.

Do you feel awkward or uncomfortable
when you're angry? Circle one: Yes.   No.   Sometimes.

When you stepped back and rested in stillness, what happened to the anger?
Circle one: Did it…   Intensify?   Fade?   Change?   Or remain the same?

Now do this exercise again, dialing your anger back to 5 percent—just a small amount of anger. Is there a benefit to knowing what your body feels like when you're just a little bit angry? Could this benefit have anything to do with emotional waves and the refractory period?

Exactly! Knowing that you're *beginning* to feel angry is an early warning system. When you notice the initial physical sensations and thoughts at the start of the anger wave, you can often make better choices than when you're really angry and caught in the refractory period.

Consider how noticing that you're beginning to feel angry, and then making a wise choice, might play out for you. List three helpful choices that you could make in almost any situation when you notice you are beginning to feel angry.

1. _____

2. _____

3. _____

If you wish, you can embody various percentages of other emotions, perhaps sadness, fear, jealousy, or excitement. I strongly encourage you to end this activity by expressing and embodying as much joy as you can.

Activity: Unpleasant Events

Often we experience intense emotional waves when we have an unpleasant experience—when things don't go our way. Take a moment to remember an unpleasant event from the last few days. It may not have been a huge deal, although it could have been. When you have an event in mind, fill out the following page.

Just a few brief words or sketches are fine. In the Thought Bubble, note the thoughts that appeared during the unpleasant event. In the Feelings Bubble, note the emotions that appeared during the event. And in the Body Bubble, note what was happening in your body and how your body *felt* during the event.

Remember, as you fill out the bubbles it may be helpful to consider your five senses—sight, hearing, taste, touch, and smell—as well as your facial expressions and physical sensations during the unpleasant event. Remember, noticing when things are unpleasant and when you are beginning to get upset can allow you to make a wise choice before you become stuck in the refractory period.

UNPLEASANT EVENT

Event: _____

Thought Bubble

Feelings Bubble

Body Bubble

Giving Yourself the Gift of Mindfulness

This chapter has been about befriending feelings and having your feelings without your feelings having you. These skills are absolutely essential for achieving peak performance and finding flow. So, for the next week or so do the following:

- Do the Befriending Feelings practice every day.

- Throughout the day, do your best to simply observe your feelings, as they come and go like waves. Be aware of

    - the very beginning of a feeling wave,

    - when you're in the refractory period and unable to see things clearly, and

    - emotional waves in yourself and others.

- At the end of each day, use the following unpleasant events calendar to record unpleasant events and how they affect you. You might want to be especially curious about whether there are themes or patterns to the events and your experience.

UNPLEASANT EVENTS CALENDAR

Day: What was the event?	What thoughts appeared during the event?	What feelings or emotions appeared during the event?	How did your body feel during the event?	What thoughts, feelings, and body sensations are present now, as you write about the event?
Monday:				
Tuesday:				
Wednesday:				

Thursday:	Friday:	Saturday:	Sunday:

CHAPTER 7

Responding Rather Than Reacting

Life is 10 percent of what happens to me and 90 percent of how I react [or respond] to it.

—Charles R. Swindoll, pastor, author, and educator

Bringing our kind and curious attention to our physical sensations, thoughts, and feelings allows us to gather the internal information that will allow us to respond (choose our behavior) rather than react (act automatically) when faced with typical athletic and personal difficulties and challenges, such as making a mistake; getting injured; being cut; or having difficulty with a teammate, coach, friend, or family member. The ability to respond rather than react has multiple benefits: it minimizes the likelihood that we will become involved in an upset or a conflict, it allows us to address upsets and conflicts calmly in real time, it decreases the chance that we will say or do something we regret, and it helps us clear things up when we do say or do something we regret. Ultimately, using this skill leaves us with more time, peace, clarity, and energy to achieve peak performance and experience flow. In this chapter we will use the analogy of "holes" and "different streets," as depicted in the poem in the following section, to bring to life the principle of responding rather than reacting.

Basic Concept: Holes and Different Streets

Please read the following poem, by Portia Nelson, slowly and twice. Bring kindness and curiosity to the thoughts and feelings that appear as you read the poem.

Autobiography in Five Short Chapters

Chapter One

I walk down the street.

There is a deep hole in the sidewalk.

I fall in.

I am lost… I am helpless.

It isn't my fault…

It takes forever to find a way out.

Chapter Two

I walk down the same street.

There is a deep hole in the sidewalk.

I pretend I don't see it.

I fall in again.

I can't believe I am in this same place.

But, it isn't my fault.

It still takes a long time to get out.

Chapter Three

I walk down the same street.

There is a deep hole in the sidewalk.

I see it is there.

I still fall in…it's a habit…but,

my eyes are open.

I know where I am.

It is my fault.

I get out immediately.

Chapter Four

I walk down the same street.

There is a deep hole in the sidewalk.

I walk around it.

Chapter Five

I walk down another street.

Now ask yourself: Is the woman who wrote the poem talking about a real street with a real hole?

Not really. She's talking about everyday problems and difficulties, especially ones that happen again and again.

In *It's Not About the Bra*, Brandi Chastain describes a moment when she acted impulsively and fell into a hole:

I was having one of those games where, as hard as I tried, my efforts weren't translating into much success on the scoreboard. We were dominating, and should have been winning, but weren't. And my frustration was growing by the minute; every miss-touch and mistake fed my anger. At one point an opponent took the ball from me, and…I simply went over the edge. In a fit of "sports rage"…I chased her down and tackled her from behind, sliding and hitting her mid-calf with two feet. I got the ball but fouled her badly in the process. Half a second later the whistle blew. Immediately the referee held the yellow card up to my face, signaling a penalty. According to the rules at the time the card meant I had to come out of the game. (2004, 3)

When viewed through the lens of mindfulness, Chastain's incredibly honest description of her inner experience may help you see how you can apply the practices in this book in your life. Mixing two metaphors, if Chastain had learned the skills of mindfulness, she might have been more aware that a wave of anger and frustration was building and then been able to choose a different street. If you were her teammate, and you noticed that she was getting frustrated, what would you have said to her to help her respond in this situation? Take a moment and come up with as many helpful sayings as you can.

_____

_____

_____

Some suggestions for short, simple phrases that you can say when a teammate is having a rough time appear below. And if you would say the phrases on this page, or the ones you came up with, to a teammate, then the next time you are feeling frustrated, angry, and about to go over the edge, you can say them to yourself.

Helpful Phrases

EASY GIRL.

WE'VE GOT TIME.

WE GOT THIS.

PLAY CLEAN.

DEEP BREATH.

Keep it simple.

TRUST.

Play like a champion.

Let it go.

Detour: anger hole...

ReSpoNd.

Don't let it get to you.

I see you're frustrated.

Practice: ABCs

The next time you realize you are in a hole, or on the verge of falling into one, do this simple practice:

A: Acknowledge the situation.

B: Breathe…

C: Choose how you will respond.

Reflection: The Power of Responding

Describe a moment during the last week when using the ABC practice or choosing a different street would have been helpful. If you are stumped, the next section offers some common examples of holes we fall into.

_____

_____

_____

_____

_____

_____

_____

Activity: Holes

Do you have problems or difficulties that seem to come up again and again? Below are common holes that many athletes fall into. Circle the ones that apply to you.

TRAINING AND COMPETITION HOLES

- Thinking about the past or future
- Believing Unkind Mind
- Being gripped by emotion
- Reacting to difficulties

TEAMMATE HOLES

- Blaming
- Poor communication
- Jealousy
- Excessive competition
- Lack of trust
- Frequent disagreements
- Excluding
- Gossiping
- Mean teasing

COMMUNICATING-WITH-YOUR-COACH HOLES

- Not listening
- Not speaking your truth
- Exaggerating or minimizing injury
- Poor communication
- Slacking off in practice
- Grumbling silently or out loud about the coach

SCHOOL AND WORK HOLES

- Procrastination
- Disorganization
- Lack of interest
- Not asking for help
- Unkind Mind attacks

FRIEND HOLES

- Feeling excluded or jealous
- Going along with something to be "cool"
- Not saying what you want
- Being mean

RISK HOLES

- Drinking
- Using drugs
- Driving unsafely
- Having unprotected sex
- Eating disorders
- Stealing
- Fighting
- Participating in gangs
- Cutting
- Suicidal thinking

RELATIONSHIP AND FAMILY HOLES

- Not listening
- Not being listened to
- Not speaking your truth
- Disagreements about responsibilities and privileges

List your top three holes—repetitive problems or difficulties.

1. _____

2. _____

3. _____

Sometimes it may feel like you have been pushed into a hole, whereas at other times you may push or drag someone else into a hole. Sometimes you can fall into a hole all by yourself. Take a look at the three holes you listed and see which of these descriptions applies to each one.

Activity: Responding, or Choosing a Different Street

Many athletes find that using the image of choosing a different street helps them respond rather than react in difficult situations. *Responding* means pausing, breathing, and choosing your behavior—in other words, intentionally walking down a different street in sports and in life. *Reacting* is acting automatically, out of habit, usually during the refractory period—in other words, falling into a hole. Together you, your coach, and your teammates may find this analogy a powerful team tool and a true game changer. For example, if a ref makes a bad call and you see a teammate getting angry, you might say, "Don't fall into the 'bad call' hole."

Using one of the top three repetitive problems or difficulties from your list, respond to the following prompts.

HOLES AND DIFFERENT STREETS

Briefly describe the hole, which is your problem or difficulty.

_____

_____

_____

List the thoughts that typically appear when you face this difficulty.

_____

_____

_____

List the feelings that typically appear when you face this difficulty.

_____

_____

_____

List at least three different streets, creative actions, or responses that you could choose that might allow you to stay out of the hole.

_____

_____

_____

Sometimes in sports and in life we aren't able to catch ourselves, and we fall into the hole. Then, all we can do is smile, forgive ourselves, make amends, learn our lessons, and begin again. This process usually involves a friendly gesture, such as helping up the opponent you just decked, offering a sincere apology, and then demonstrating that you've learned your lesson by playing clean. We will consider these topics again in chapter 9, "Mistakes, Self-Compassion, and Intentions."

Giving Yourself the Gift of Mindfulness

While it may seem simple, noticing holes and choosing different streets is harder than it sounds. Doing so is also a true game changer. So, for the next week, or month, commit to

- noticing holes;

- consciously practicing responding (choosing a different street) rather than reacting (falling into the hole); and,

- if you can't find a different street, at the very least sitting down on the sidewalk, pausing, and considering your options.

As you come to the end of part 1, take a moment to congratulate yourself. If you have read the book from the beginning, listened to the recorded practices, done the exercises, and begun to apply the principles in your daily life, then you are well on your way to mastering the fundamentals of mindfulness. By practicing these skills, you have increased your ability to approach your physical, mental, and emotional experience with kindness and curiosity. These skills lay the foundation for bringing mindfulness into action, and for responding rather than reacting in the heat of the moment during training, competition, and daily life.

As you continue to develop your mindfulness skills, you may find it inspiring to know that although she may not have used the term "mindfulness," Brandi Chastain utilized these skills at the 1999 World Cup. She provides a powerful example of putting *all* the skills you are practicing into action, in front of eighty thousand spectators, at one of the most competitive events in the world:

We walked through the shadowy tunnel at Giant's Stadium in New Jersey for the opening game and stepped into the bright sunlight. A huge roar burst from the capacity crowd. The flashing of thousands of cameras exploded before our eyes, and the smell of fresh cut grass was in the air [Mindfulness of the present moment—sights, sounds, and smells.]...

I was flooded by a rush of anxiety. Oh my God, I have to perform, I realized. I was paralyzed with thoughts I had never had before on a soccer field. What if I can't hold up my end? What if I don't live up to the expectations of my teammates, or myself? [Mindfulness of feelings and thoughts.]

I actually began to shake. [Mindfulness of physical sensations.]

I found my refocusing technique. I bent down and pulled up my socks, one of the gestures we had learned to signify leaving the past moments behind and getting into the new one. [A mindful choice to return to the body and the present moment.] (2004, 176)

PART 2

Advanced Skills—Integration

Part 1 covered the basics of mindfulness and the fundamental skills for finding flow in sports and in life. The following chapters cover more advanced and challenging topics. As with progressive physical drills, the following practices will have you use mental and emotional "muscles" in new and unusual ways. Simply notice if you think a practice seems crazy, too hard, useless, or impossible. And then, as Nike says, "Just do it!" and see what happens. As it is with making specific physical changes to posture, alignment, or technique, there may be a period of awkwardness, and even frustration, before you realize the full benefits of a new practice.

You can always choose to skip a particular practice, or come back to it later. And choose wisely. It may be that you are truly not ready for a practice, that you need to develop your core mindfulness skills before you are able to do these more advanced practices, or it may be that, like the athlete in the first image in the "Wise Effort and Injury Prevention" section (chapter 4), you are cheating yourself by staying in your comfort zone.

CHAPTER 8

Facing Challenges

Sports are more than just games. They're about life, emotion, passion, and some of the greatest highs and lows we can experience.

—Unknown

If you've been reading this book from the beginning, you already have a powerful set of tools to help you live a less stressful, more enjoyable life. Here's a quick review. You've learned to rest in stillness and quietness and you've practiced tuning in to your body, watching your thoughts, befriending your feelings, learning to ride the waves of your emotions, and responding (taking a different street) rather than reacting (falling into the same old holes).

In this chapter you will learn simple practices and principles for responding to challenges and rebounding from setbacks, such as losing your cell phone and having a rough practice, to dealing with more extreme problems, such as getting injured, losing your starting spot, being cut, dealing with an unexpected coaching change, ending a relationship, experiencing difficulties at school or work, or even grieving the death of a teammate or family member.

Often a wise and kind first step is simply to befriend your feelings of upset, disappointment, anger, jealousy, fear, despair, and doubt by doing the Befriending Feelings practice in chapter 6.

Practice: PEACE

You can download an audio recording of this practice at http://www.newharbinger.com/40217.

This PEACE practice will support you as you face challenges in sports and in life. If you practice it repeatedly, you'll remember the basic elements and naturally tune in to the aspects of the practice that will be most helpful in a given situation. As you have already discovered, mindfulness is much more than just watching the breath. For me, the power and beauty of mindfulness is that it helps me when things are most difficult.

PEACE is an acronym for a practice that can be used in any difficult situation. As you do this practice for the first time, bring to mind a current problem that you're experiencing. If possible, choose something small to begin with—a minor difficulty. If you are dealing with something more intense, take your time, go slow, be gentle, and seek support if you need it. Let's begin.

- **P** *is for pause. When you realize that things are difficult, pause.*

- **E** *is for exhale. When you exhale, you may want to let out a sigh or a groan. You may even want to cry. That's okay. And after you exhale, you want to…? Inhale. Just keep breathing.…*

- **A** *is for acknowledge, accept, and allow. As you continue to breathe, acknowledge the situation as it is. Maybe your backpack with all your stuff is gone, you just blew your ACL, or your new un-best friend is now dating your new ex. Acknowledging a situation doesn't mean you're happy about it. It just means that you recognize the situation is what it is, whether you like it or not.…* **A** *is also for accept—accepting the situation and your reaction to it, whether you're feeling furious, devastated, heartbroken, jealous, all of the above, or something else entirely.… Finally,* **A** *is for allowing your experience. Do your best to rest in the Still Quiet Place and just watch all of your thoughts, feelings, and body sensations. Notice if you're tempted to suppress your experience by pretending that you're fine. Notice if you want to create additional drama by rehashing things in your head or with friends. See if you can allow these tendencies too. Do your best to discover a middle way—a way of having your thoughts and feelings without your thoughts and feelings having you and making you act in ways you may regret.*

- **C** *is for choose. When you're ready—and this may take a few moments, hours, days, weeks, or even months, depending on the situation—choose how you'll respond. At its best, responding involves some additional Cs: clarity, courage, compassion, and comedy. Clarity is being clear about what you want, what your limits are, and what you're responsible for. Courage means bravely speaking your truth and hearing the truth of others. Compassion means being kind toward yourself and others and understanding how incredibly difficult it sometimes is to be a human being. As for comedy, the word "humor" might be a better fit, but it doesn't start with C.… It's amazing how helpful it can be to have a sense of humor and to not take yourself or your situation too seriously.*

- **E** *is for engage. After you've paused, exhaled, allowed your experience, and chosen your response, you're ready to engage with people, with the situation, and with life.*

Now that you've practiced PEACE, you can use the practice in other real-life situations. For extreme circumstances, you may need to repeat the practice several times a day, and you may also want to seek support from a friend, a parent, a coach, a counselor, or a doctor.

The following anonymous quote beautifully summarizes the essence of the PEACE practice:

Peace. It does not mean to be in a place where there is no noise, trouble, or hard work. It means to be in the midst of those things and still be calm in your heart.

Practice: Befriending Physical Pain

Previously you learned how to befriend feelings or emotions. Now, you can use the same practice to work with physical pain. Typically, in our culture we are taught to take medication, do physical therapy, or have surgery to eliminate pain. Each of these approaches has its time and place and can be extremely valuable and effective. However, despite our best efforts and the best efforts of our coaches, trainers, massage therapists, acupuncturists, physical therapists, physicians, and surgeons, sometimes the pain remains.

Interestingly the pioneering scientific studies on mindfulness were done with patients who had been living with chronic pain for an average of seven years and had received all the recommended conventional medical interventions—meds, physical therapy, and surgery. When these people were taught mindfulness, they had less pain or greater ability to cope with their pain, or both. They were less stressed, depressed, and anxious. Their medication usage decreased, and they were able to live with greater joy and sense of purpose.

Just as you learned to do with intense emotions, these patients learned to turn toward their physical pain with kindness and curiosity. They took time to simply breathe and be with their pain without trying to change it or fix it. They did this gently—breathing, feeling the physical sensations in their bodies, and noticing the "color," "texture," intensity, and ebb and flow of the variety of sensations we label as "pain." Observing pain with kindness and curiosity is a powerful tool that can actually change your relationship with pain.

And as with befriending emotions and physical stretching and training, it is important to know when to back off and choose to attend to other aspects of your experience. As a counterbalance to attending to pain, it can be helpful to rest your attention on and appreciate the areas of your body that aren't in pain—where the ear connects with the head, the crease of the elbow or knee, the spaces between the fingers—or to shift your attention from your body outward to the sights and sounds of your surroundings.

Often when we experience pain we resist it. In addition to bringing our kind and curious attention to our pain, noticing the ever-changing details of our experience—the aching, throbbing, stabbing, easing, increasing, and diminishing—then focusing on areas of our bodies that are in comfort and ease and shifting our focus outward, we can also practice accepting the pain rather than resisting it. As you will learn in the next section, *accepting* doesn't mean that we don't do everything within reason to address the pain; accepting simply means we don't waste our energy and increase our suffering by resisting what we can't change. Together the practices in this section—paying attention to the sensations of pain with kindness and curiosity, paying attention to the areas of the body that aren't in pain, and accepting pain—can support you in developing your capacity to *be with* pain without being consumed by it.

Activity: Suffering = Pain x Resistance

Here's something you may have already discovered for yourself: much of the suffering related to a painful or unpleasant event is due to our thoughts and feelings about the event. And much of that thinking and feeling emphasizes the past or, more often, the future: *I really screwed up that last sequence* expands into *I always screw up. I lost my starting spot* becomes *I'll never start again. This pain is intense* solidifies into *This pain will always be unbearable.* The essence of most of this upsetting thinking and feeling is resistance; put simply, resistance is wanting things to be different than they actually are.

The following mathematical equation from Shinzen Young (2011) may help you understand this connection:

Suffering = Pain x Resistance

If you are dealing with either physical or emotional pain, the equation probably makes sense exactly as it is written. If you are dealing with other unpleasant situations, you can think of *suffering* as the intensity of your upset, *pain* as unpleasantness, and *resistance* as how much you want things to be different.

In other words, when something unpleasant happens, how upset you are depends not only on what happened, but also on how much you want things to be different. Often, though not always, the level of pain (or unpleasantness) is fixed and cannot be changed and the only part of the equation we can adjust is our resistance (how much we want things to be different).

Let's make this more real with a couple of examples. Perhaps you blew out your ACL. For most athletes that would be a 9 on a pain scale of 1 to 10 (with 1 being very little pain and 10 being extreme pain). The injury is both physically and emotionally painful. You can't change that. However, your level of suffering is at least partially within your control. Wallowing in level-9 resistance—*The ref should have had better control of the game. That player should have been called on her fouls and fouled out earlier. This is so unfair. This shouldn't have happened*—results in a suffering score of 81. Whereas decreasing your resistance to 2—*Injury is part of the game. I am going to rock rehab and bounce back from this*—results in a suffering score of 18.

Or say that, for you, not making the regional team is a 7 on the pain scale. Resisting the outcome with thoughts like *The selection process was political and unfair* might be a 7 on the resistance scale. So in this scenario, your level of suffering is 49. A different way of thinking, such as *I am really disappointed, and I'm going to work hard and try again*, might have a lower resistance score, say 3. This thinking doesn't change the pain of not making the team, but it does decrease the intensity of your suffering from 49 to 21. And an added bonus is that usually this less resistive, more accepting type of thinking gives you a way to move forward—a wise next step, a specific action to take.

Many athletes find this equation really helpful when dealing with painful situations. As you read this book, you may be working with a profoundly painful situation, such as a serious injury, financial hardship, the end of a relationship, or an illness or death in your family. In such cases, to honor your experience you may increase the pain scale. If you're dealing with an extremely painful situation, take some time to rest in stillness and tenderly acknowledge the pain… Go easy… Be gentle.

Remember that wanting things to be different increases suffering or upset. Accepting things as they are, no matter how terrible, helps us choose our next sane and joyful step (more on this below), such as doubling down on our rehab efforts, recommitting to working on specific skills and drills, refining our technique, talking to the coach to get feedback, or seeking out support for ourselves or a family member. As Jim Afremow writes, "Rather than viewing adversity as a sign that things are getting worse, be inspired by the opportunity to make your game better. The choice is whether to allow adversity to become a hindrance to your game or to use it to make yourself stronger" (2013, 100).

As you work with this practice it is important to remember a few things:

- Wanting things to be different isn't bad or wrong; it's very natural.

- Accepting things the way they are doesn't necessarily mean giving up and not doing anything to change the situation.

- If your pain score is higher than 10, seek support from a friend, counselor, therapist, coach, religious leader, or doctor.

Basic Concept: Humor

As mentioned in the PEACE practice, comedy, or humor, can bring lightness to difficult moments. A great example of incorporating humor into a precompetition ritual (chapter 4) comes from Canadian Olympic swimmer Santo Condorelli. He actually gives his dad the finger before every race. This ritual began when Condorelli was a scrawny eight-year-old swimmer and felt "scared ****less" standing on the starting blocks next to much bigger guys who had matured earlier than he had. So his dad said, "When you get on the blocks, just put everything out of your mind and swim like there's nobody near you." Condorelli asked him how he could do that, and his dad responded, "Well, you say '**** it'" (Bowmile 2016). At the start of the next race Condorelli gave his dad the finger from the blocks, and this subsequently became his prerace ritual. He found that it calmed his nerves and allowed him to concentrate. After creating this ritual he began to win races.

It should be noted that this ritual has not been without controversy. In 2010 at the Speedo Junior National Championships, television cameras captured Condorelli's signature move. Some people were offended, and some took it personally. He has since modified his ritual slightly. Now he simply puts his middle finger on his forehead rather than extending his arm up in the air. It is the same gesture but draws less attention.

I am not suggesting you adopt this particular gesture, but I am encouraging you to find the precompetition ritual and mistake ritual (chapter 9) that help you (and your teammates) lighten up and take yourself less seriously and get your head in the game (chapter 5).

While humorous rituals are helpful, sometimes it is a spontaneous comment or gesture that will allow you and your teammates to lighten up. Consider LeBron James's comment to Channing Frye, who was struggling after the recent deaths of his parents:

> During a game midway through the season, I was completely lost emotionally. I wasn't smiling. I wasn't enjoying the game. I was just going through the motions. LeBron noticed that I was withdrawn, and he walked over to me during a timeout.
>
> "Channing," he said.
>
> I snapped out of my daze for a moment and looked over at Bron. He looked really serious. No expression.
>
> And then he said…
>
> "Did you just fart?"
>
> I couldn't help but laugh. Everyone knows I love a good fart joke! Everyone on the team…knows how to pull me out of a funk. (Frye 2017)

For humor to be effective, it is important that you *read* your teammates and wisely choose what you say. Sometimes funny and lighthearted is the way to go, but at other times fierce "I've got your back" support is needed. If you and your teammates tend to get tightly wound, introducing lighthearted humor can help all of you find flow.

Basic Concept: Good News, Bad News, Who Knows?

As the saying goes, "S--t happens." Events occur… *Then* we have all sorts of thoughts about them… Then we believe the thoughts… Then we have feelings about the thoughts we believe…and these thoughts and feelings color how we see and respond to the situation. So, it can be helpful to remain curious and open, and to hold our experience lightly.

Every athlete's career is a series of events that we typically believe are "good news" or "bad news." Here is an example:

> You get invited to play for your dream team.
>
> Most of your family and friends say, "This is such good news! Congratulations! That's awesome!" Your grandmother says, "Good news, bad news, who knows?"

On your first day of training, you are injured. Most of your family and friends say, "Oh no, this is such bad news! That's terrible." Your grandmother says, "Good news, bad news, who knows?"

You get a slower start to the season. Late in the season, the national team is looking to fill out the roster. Many potential candidates are exhausted or injured. And you are just coming in to good form. You get called up.

Most of your family and friends exclaim, "This is wonderful news. That's so exciting!" And of course your grandmother smiles and says, "Good news, bad news, who knows?"

Can you remember a time when you were convinced that something was terrible? Have you ever been in a situation when a whole team—players, coaches, parents—all began telling the same story? For example, "The new director of coaching is an idiot." "Without our star we are going to lose." On the flip side, can you recall a time when you thought something was going to be great? *We got an easy team in the first round of the tournament. The coach likes me.*

As you probably realized during the Thought Watching practice (chapter 5), each of us has thousands of thoughts a day. And not only do we have these thoughts, but we also generally *believe* them, take them personally, and categorize them as good news or bad news. Perhaps a more useful approach would be to bring our kind and curious attention to the situation and rest in "Who knows?"

Is there a place in your sports life, or in you daily life, where you are currently telling a story that something is terrible? Or great?

_____

_____

_____

_____

When you view the situation without the story, what do you discover?

_____

_____

_____

_____

Are you willing to take a bold leap and consider that the situation is, as the wise woman, author, and teacher Byron Katie says, "happening for you not to you"?

Basic Concept: It Is Happening for Me, Not to Me.

What does "It is happening for me, not to me" actually mean? When we believe that something we categorize as bad news has happened "to" us, we often wallow in negative thinking. *The selection process was unfair. That bad call cost us the game. This injury has ruined my life.* After a natural period of disappointment, or even grief, true champions use adversity to learn and grow. They take the hand they have been dealt and play it to the best of their ability. As a young gymnast, I suffered from chronic shoulder dislocations. So in the seventh grade I chose to have surgery to rebuild my right shoulder, and then in the eighth grade I had the same surgery on my left shoulder. After the surgeries I chose to go to the gym every day in a sling, to do conditioning, to work on strength and flexibility, and to practice dance elements. When my shoulders had healed I had elegant, dynamic, powerful leap sequences. Not only was my body (except for my arms) stronger and more flexible, but my heart and mind were stronger and more flexible too. Rather than getting down, I chose to use the challenge of repeated injury, and surgery, to discover and develop resilience—the ability to bounce back.

Brandi Chastain beautifully describes this particular way of working with adversity in her powerful "Letter to My Younger Self." You may benefit from reading this inspiring letter frequently, especially when you are feeling down. Here is just part of the wisdom she shares in the letter:

> You're going to be humbled by injuries. Two ACL tears and a meniscus tear will keep you from the game you love for almost two-and-a-half years. Be patient. Listen to your body. This time away will give you a chance to pause—to experience what it's like to not be a starter, to not be the one who scored a goal or who made an impact. You will learn to appreciate your teammates. They will carry on while you cheer from the sideline. They, in turn, will grow to appreciate you more. They will cheer you on as you work your way back into the lineup.
>
> The mental and physical challenges of rehabbing your body will test your patience. Have faith in those moments—they will define your future perseverance. No athlete knows what's on the other side of significant injuries. Live all of your questions and trust the process. You'll return a better player, a better teammate, a better person. (2015)

Looking back, Chastain can see how the injury happened for her. Because of the injury she learned to be humble, to appreciate her teammates, to receive support, to persevere, to improve her self-care, and to tune in to her body and mind.

Basic Concept: This Too Shall Pass—Impermanence and Equanimity

Another way of dealing with good news and bad news is to remember that all experiences are impermanent—the highs of mastering a new skill, making the team, and winning the championship, and the lows of a slump, of an injury, of being cut, and of losing. Remembering that all experiences are temporary allows us to delight in the highs and move through the lows without letting either go to our heads, making us cocky or depressed. A word for this balanced approach is "equanimity."

Equanimity is having mental or emotional stability, or composure, especially in challenging moments; it's a sense of calmness and equilibrium. Success and failure, winning and losing, progress and setbacks are all part of sport and life. Practicing equanimity—resting in stillness and quietness, allowing physical sensations, thoughts, and feelings to arise and pass away during practice and competition (especially before and after high-profile events)—will help you perform to the best of your ability.

Betsey Armstrong, 2008 Olympic silver medalist in water polo, uses the saying "Keep calm and carry on." She says "a challenging time is just that—a period in time. Taking a few deep breaths and knowing that it won't last forever really allows me to focus on the present moment and task at hand" (Women's Health 2012).

The value and necessity of practicing equanimity in the face of both tremendous success and devastating failure, and also of discovering who you are beyond your identity as an athlete (For more on this, see "Reflection: Beyond Competition," chapter 13) is becoming increasingly clear, especially as more and more athletes (including Olympic medalists such as Michael Phelps, Allison Schmitt, and Margaux Isaksen) open up about their experiences with depression (Florio and Shapiro 2016; Block 2016). Multi-record-setting MLB player Shawn Green writes about this balance:

> Just as I didn't want to dwell for long about a bad at-bat, I didn't want to allow myself to get too caught up in home runs either. The victorious jog around the bases was plenty... Becoming attached to success is just as dangerous as becoming attached to failure. (2011, 124)

Basic Concept: Faith, Patience, and Perseverance

As a young gymnast, I came across a poem by an unknown author that helped me during rough times. In fact, the poem was so useful that I memorized it, and I remember almost all of it by heart all these years later. Here's the poem. Although it refers to a gymnast, it applies to athletes in any sport.

Patience is man's greatest virtue,
or so the saying goes.
A gymnast must have said it,
for a gymnast surely knows,
that in this funny sport of ours,
discouragement runs high,
and at times the very best will find
this virtue's passed her by.
When hands are ripped and throbbing,
and every muscle's sore,
can a gymnast still have patience,
to limp back in for more?
Can you admit you're frightened,
yet not give in to fears?
Can you conquer pain, frustrations,
and often even tears?
When someone else does something
you've tried so long to do,
can you feel really glad for her
and not just pity you?
And when you've lost old moves
you used to do,
and progress seems so slow,
can you still have faith in better days
and not feel so sad and low?
And when success seems so far away,
your efforts all in vain,
can you force yourself to wear a smile
and disregard the pain?
If despite these tribulations,
you can say, "I won't give in,"
Someday you will discover
that it's now your turn to WIN.

Now from a mindfulness perspective, there are a few useful edits we can make. We don't need to conquer pain, frustration, and tears; we can learn to have them without them having us. There is no need to force a smile. It is perhaps more helpful to acknowledge and befriend your disappointment. Then your smile will return naturally in its own time. Rather than disregarding pain, it is wiser to bring your kind and curious attention to the sensations in your body and learn to recognize the difference between the normal aches and pains of training and the more serious signals of injury and overtraining. And it may be wise to expand the definition of winning. We can *choose* to define winning as more than the fastest time, the number flashed by the judges, or the score on the scoreboard. For example, after my shoulder surgeries, it was definitely a win when I could finally hold up my gradually healing arm long enough to put my hair in a ponytail! Winning can be mastering a skill alone in a gym; holding your tongue when taunted by an opponent; playing until the whistle, even when the scoreboard says you lost; and, of course, it can be lifting and kissing the medal or trophy.

For the next week or so, using the expanded definition of "winning" just described, every night before you go to sleep track your wins with the worksheet on the following page, or create a list on your phone or in an online document.

DAILY WINS

Day	Wins
Monday	1. 2. 3.
Tuesday	1. 2. 3.
Wednesday	1. 2. 3.
Thursday	1. 2. 3.
Friday	1. 2. 3.
Saturday	1. 2. 3.
Sunday	1. 2. 3.

Activity: Next Sane and Joyful Step

Whether you are winning in the conventional sense, or the expanded sense, or you are struggling and feeling overwhelmed and uncertain, it can be helpful to consider what Coach G calls "your next sane and joyful step." When we find ourselves in a good news or a bad news story, often we can get waaaay ahead of ourselves, lost in our fantasies or nightmares about the future. When you notice yourself spinning into the future, breathe, come back to this moment, check in with yourself, honestly assess the situation, and then ask yourself, "What is my next sane and joyful step?" This step is a simple, doable present-moment action.

Choosing our next sane and joyful step sometimes requires taking a hard look at ourselves and acknowledging our weaknesses or blind spots. Sometimes it means hearing things that we don't really want to hear from teammates or coaches. And almost always, our willingness to humbly, fearlessly face the current reality is what actually allows us to move forward.

Your next sane and joyful step could be physical, mental, emotional, spiritual, or relational; examples include shooting one hundred layups, one hundred three-pointers, and one hundred free throws, every day; bringing your attention fully into the present moment with each stoppage in play; practicing equanimity; resting in stillness and quietness; trusting "it is happening for you"; truly celebrating a particular accomplishment; or having a conversation with your coach for clarification and understanding.

In order to fulfill your commitment to yourself, it is helpful to write down your next sane and joyful step; you may want to write it below, or enter it as a daily or weekly reminder in your phone.

Next Sane and Joyful Step

_____

_____

Of course, s--t happens, challenges arise, and things change. So you will want to revisit your next sane and joyful step frequently, and you may want to make a habit of reviewing and modifying it at the beginning of each month. Next, we will consider this principle of the next sane and joyful step in the context of a pivotal time in every athlete's career.

Basic Concept: Quitting or Transitioning

There comes a time in every athlete's career where the next sane and joyful step is to accept that she or he is no longer able to play and compete at the same level. This moment may be the result of injury, aging, life circumstances (such as getting a new job or having a baby), being cut, or simply choosing to take all that you have learned about finding flow and applying it to another passion. Sometimes we get to choose the when and the why of our transitions, and sometimes we don't.

However, we always get to choose *how* we transition, and that begins with the story we tell ourselves. We have a cultural story about *quitting*, and the long and the short of it is that quitting is "bad"; quitting is a sign of weakness. We rarely speak about the healthy process of *choosing* to transition—to a less competitive league, another sport, a coaching role, being a recreational athlete, or a new passion or phase of life. While it may be this week or many years until you transition from your current level, it is important to remember that no matter how it goes down, you get to practice PEACE and write your own story.

Again, there are many ways to transition. You may want to begin noticing how friends, teammates, and famous athletes move through the various phases in their careers. Sometimes the first step in transitioning is hearing things we don't want to hear, taking what is known as a good hard look at ourselves, which I prefer to call bringing our kind, curious, and honest attention to our abilities and the situation as it is, in this moment. Some athletes have truly ugly transitions—public tantrums, huge drama, negative publicity, legal troubles, and even arrests, whereas others transition with enormous humility and grace, bringing all they have gained through sports to their next adventures.

Draymond Green, of the Golden State Warriors, recalls the wisdom about transitioning that he received from his high school coach. While Green and his Saginaw High teammates were sitting in the bleachers one day listening to assistant coach Bruce Simmons, he threw a basketball so high it almost touched the ceiling. "And the ball came down—bounce, bounce, bounce, bounce, bounce," Green recalls, "and then it rolled away." Coach Simmons then said, "That was your career. One day the ball is going to stop bouncing. What are you going to have to fall back on?" Green describes the impact this message had on him. "It's important because we in the NBA call it [the inevitable ending of one's career] Father Time, and Father Time is undefeated... It's going to catch up to us all one day. And what's next...is very, very important" (Peterson 2016).

The following stories illustrate four very unique end-of-career circumstances: a world-class athlete retiring twice—once mindlessly, and once mindfully; a potential Olympian mindfully accepting being cut; and a likely Olympian mindfully choosing to pursue other dreams.

Michael Phelps had a less-than-healthy first retirement in 2012. He experienced severe post-Olympic depression, began drinking, and went through rehab to discover who he really was beyond his identity as a multitime Olympic medalist (see "Beyond Competition," chapter 13, to spare yourself this particular agony). His first transition experience *happened for him, not to him*, and prepared him for a healthier transition in 2016. After his "final" gold medal relay swim in Rio, he said, "It's not the end of a career, it's the beginning of a new journey" (Ward-Henninger 2016).

Cassidy Lichtman devoted years of her life to making the Olympic volleyball team but did not make the final 2016 roster. Here is an abbreviated version of her thoughts about her transition:

I'm not going to the Olympics…

But at some point, as the days have gone by, I realized that I'm still me… Who I am has already been defined, not by the rosters I've made or the medals hanging in my room, but by the way I tried to approach every day—ready to work, to learn, and to serve my team in any way I could.

I gave everything—*everything*—I had, in the pursuit of this dream. And I say that not with bitterness but with conviction and with pride…

And as for me—this isn't where my story ends. This was just one chapter. One surreal, challenging, fantastic chapter. Now it's time to write the next one. (2016)

A more unusual example of transitioning comes from Stanford gymnast Elizabeth Price. In 2013 she was the number one gymnast in the world. Then she shocked the gymnastics world by choosing to end her elite international career, skipping the 2014 Gymnastics World Championship, removing herself from consideration for the 2016 Rio Olympic games, and accepting a scholarship at Stanford (Stickells 2015). Although numerous people begged her to continue to compete through the Olympics, Price *knew* in her heart that competing at Stanford, rather than in the Olympics, was her next sane and joyful step.

Michigan sports psychologist Dr. Scott Goldman notes that athletes who overidentify with their sport can lose a sense of who they are. As a result, they may feel lost and depressed when they transition: "It's easier to say, 'I *am* a swimmer' than 'I *was* a swimmer.'" In his practice he reminds athletes that

the skills and personality traits that they possess, that pushed them and propelled them to such excellence in the domain of sport, are transferable. If they find something else that they love, then they can transfer all of that passion and work ethic, grit, and resilience and creativity and adaptability into their next phase of interest. (Florio and Shapiro 2016)

Take a moment now and list five qualities you have developed through sports that will serve you and the world once you are no longer a competitive athlete.

1. _____

2. _____

3. _____

4. _____

5. _____

Remember, every transition is an opportunity to learn and grow, to bring our kind and curious attention to what will bring us joy, to develop our unique skills and talents, to consider what is needed in the world, and, ultimately, to share our gifts and be of service.

Giving Yourself the Gift of Mindfulness

Hopefully, you can see how the practices in this section support you in *applying* the PEACE practice. Acknowledging how resistance increases suffering can allow you to move toward acceptance. Accepting things as they are, even if you don't like them; maintaining a sense of humor, a "Who knows?" and "it's happening for me" attitude; and remembering that experiences are impermanent will help you develop equanimity, faith, patience, and perseverance. And these qualities create a solid foundation for the last step in the PEACE practice—choosing your next sane and joyful step, engaging, and moving forward.

When faced with difficulties:

■ Practice PEACE

■ Accept the situation and your initial reaction

■ Maintain a "Who knows?" attitude and a sense of humor

■ Remember that it is happening for you, and that this, too, shall pass

■ Choose your next sane and joyful step

CHAPTER 9

Mistakes, Self-Compassion, and Intentions

What do you do with a mistake: recognize it, admit it, learn from it, forget it.

—Dean Smith, US Olympic men's basketball coach

As athletes and human beings, we all make mistakes—lots of them; it is part of life. And as with the challenges discussed in the previous section, when we make mistakes we get to choose how we respond. Do we beat ourselves up, or pick ourselves up? In this chapter you will create a simple mistake ritual to use in the heat of the moment, practice the extremely powerful skill of self-compassion, consider a new way of completing the phrase "There's a winner and a…," and explore the distinction between setting goals and setting intentions.

Activity: Mistake Rituals

The ability to acknowledge a mistake, note self-critical thinking, and then reset is essential during practice and in the heat of competition. You can usually accomplish this process quickly with a simple mistake ritual. In *Elevating Your Game: Becoming a Triple-Impact Competitor*, Jim Thompson (2011), director of the Positive Coaching Alliance, describes three quick, effective mistake rituals: flush (making a flushing motion), no sweat (wiping sweat from the brow), and brush it off (lightly brushing the shoulder).

Alternatively, you can create your own ritual. My daughter developed a ritual based on a funny family moment. When my son was three, I walked into a closet and found him sitting on the floor, cutting the foam from dry-cleaning hangers into little pieces with children's scissors. When I asked him, "J, honey, what are you doing?" He responded, "Cutting slack." So when my daughter made a mistake in soccer, her ritual was to make a simple scissorlike motion with her index and middle finger, cutting herself slack.

Such rituals can help you release your attention from the previous play and return it to the immediate here and now of competition. Phil Jackson, champion NBA basketball player and coach, emphasizes the benefits of this process:

> Basketball takes place at such a lightning pace that it's easy to make mistakes and get obsessed with what just happened or what might happen next, which distracts you from the only thing that really matters—this very moment. (2014, 53)

You can increase the power of these quick rituals by sharing them with a supportive teammate, coach, or parent via eye contact or a simple smile. A ritual can help you lighten up; remember that mistakes are part of the game and part of the learning process; and, more importantly, achieve the crucial mental reset that lets you return your full attention to the game and find flow.

Activity: Self-Esteem

Self-esteem, how we think about ourselves, has two main elements. First, there's how we think about ourselves compared to others: *I am better than or worse than you.* Second, there's how we think about ourselves in terms of success and failure: *I'm a good—successful—student, athlete, friend, person*, or *I'm a bad—failing—student, athlete, friend, person.*

Self-esteem *seems* great when we're on the upside—thinking we're better than someone else or feeling successful. However, being on the downside of self-esteem can be like pouring gasoline on the fire of Unkind Mind.

Let's do a little experiment to see how self-esteem works. Start by bringing to mind a time when you felt successful or better than someone else. Recall the situation in detail, and then briefly describe it here.

_____

_____

What thoughts did you have in the situation?

_____

_____

What feelings did you have in the situation?

_____

_____

How did these thoughts and feelings show up in your body?

_____

_____

(If you're not sure, here's a hint: when I feel successful or better than others, I have a bit of swagger, my head is high, and my chest is literally a bit puffed up.)

Now do the same thing with the downside of self-esteem. Bring to mind a time when you felt like a failure or like you were worse than someone else. Recall the situation in detail, and then briefly describe it here.

_____

_____

What thoughts did you have in the situation?

_____

_____

What feelings did you have in the situation?

_____

_____

How did these thoughts and feelings show up in your body?

_____

_____

(Again, here's a hint: when I feel like a failure or worse than others, my body is a bit deflated and caved in.)

Now list three traits that give you high self-esteem.

1. _____

2. _____

3. _____

Now consider whether your high self-esteem, or pride related to these traits, has a downside. For example, do you feel stressed out when you don't act, behave, or perform as you or others expect? Here are some examples that may clarify this concept:

Trait: *I am tough.*

Downsides: *Sometimes it's exhausting to be tough. Sometimes I want to be supported and comforted. Sometimes my toughness is covering my pain.*

Trait: *I am awesome at free throws.*

Downsides: *Sometimes I get cocky. Sometimes when I miss it messes with my head.*

Trait: *I am nice.*

Downsides: *Sometimes I don't take good care of myself. Sometimes I do things I don't want to do.*

Every trait has a downside and an upside. What are the downsides of the three traits you listed that give you high self-esteem?

1. _____

2. _____

3. _____

The good news is, it's possible to ride the roller coaster of better than versus worse than and success versus failure without taking it all quite so seriously. We can learn to truly enjoy our strengths and successes, and accept our weaknesses and so-called failures, without letting them define who we think we are. We can learn to hold both "up" and "down" experiences lightly, with kindness and curiosity. It is helpful to remember the concept of impermanence, that the experiences of feeling successful or better than others, as well as the experiences of feeling like a failure or worse than others, are temporary, and they don't define us.

Practice: Self-Compassion

Self-compassion is based on the understanding that all human beings, including you, have difficulty, and that all human beings, including you, deserve kindness. Unlike self-esteem, self-compassion doesn't depend on what you think of yourself, your successes or failures, or how you compare to others.

According to Dr. Kristin Neff (2011), a pioneer and respected researcher in the field of self-compassion, there are three parts to self-compassion: mindful awareness, self-kindness, and an understanding of our common humanity. Hopefully, at this point in the book, it's clear that the Still Quiet Place is all about mindful awareness and kindness! Still, let's consider how Dr. Neff describes these two qualities. To paraphrase, she says that mindful awareness means being willing to observe negative thoughts and emotions with openness and clarity and without suppressing or indulging them. And she describes self-kindness as offering ourselves kindness, especially when we suffer, fail, or feel inadequate.

The third element of self-compassion is understanding our common humanity, recognizing that suffering and feelings of personal inadequacy are part of the human experience. Every athlete and every human being has times when they feel sad, mad, afraid, upset, jealous, insecure, and disappointed; these experiences don't just happen to you and you alone. In other words, we all feel bad about ourselves sometimes.

So take a moment now to revisit the previous activity, remembering the situation you wrote down when you felt you were worse than someone else or you were a failure. Recall this situation in as much detail as possible. Let the thoughts and feelings from the experience bubble up… Now, rest your hand on your chest (feel how your body responds to this simple touch) and say these words:

> *It was really rough when* [fill in the blank]. *Everyone goes through tough times. In this moment, I offer myself kindness and compassion.*

How does it feel to offer kindness to yourself in this way?

_____

_____

If this practice feels weird or awkward, that's okay. As with other new skills, the more you practice the more natural offering yourself kindness and compassion will become. So whenever you're having a rough time, *practice* offering yourself the same kindness and compassion you'd offer a true friend.

According to Dr. Neff, self-compassion doesn't just increase well-being; it also increases our resilience (our ability to get through hard times, to bounce back) and our motivation to improve our performance after difficult events (Breines and Chen 2012). In fact, her research showed that practicing self-compassion increased college students' ability to deal with perceived academic failure (Neff, Hsieh, and Dejitterat 2005). Related research suggests that as an athlete, you can experience specific benefits from practicing self-compassion:

- Young women athletes with naturally higher self-compassion were less likely to experience shame, social physique (body) anxiety, fear of failure, and fear of negative evaluation (Mosewich et al. 2011).

- Female athletes reported that self-compassion was advantageous in difficult sports-specific situations because it decreased rumination (obsessive, negative thinking) and increased positivity and perseverance (Ferguson et al. 2014).

- Women athletes with higher self-compassion levels generally responded in healthier ways to emotionally difficult hypothetical and recalled situations in sports (being responsible for losing a game and worst sports experience) than their less self-compassionate counterparts. Higher self-compassion was associated with lower negative affect (emotion), fewer catastrophizing thoughts (thinking the worst will happen), fewer personalizing thoughts (focusing on oneself), and higher behavioral equanimity (Reis et al. 2015).

- More importantly, research shows that self-compassion, like mindfulness, is a learnable skill; female varsity athletes who initially self-identified as self-critical and then learned self-compassion more effectively managed self-criticism, rumination (obsessive thinking), and concern about mistakes. The researchers concluded that fostering a self-compassionate frame of mind is a potential coping mechanism for female athletes dealing with negative events in sports (Mosewich et al. 2013).

For you guys who may be thinking, *Well, self-compassion is great for female athletes, but it's not for me*, it may help you to know that the studies showing the benefits of self-compassion for academic failure were done with men and women; members of the US men's national BMX team learned self-compassion during the mindfulness performance enhancement, awareness, and knowledge (mPEAK) training (see "The Benefits of Mindfulness" section, chapter 2); the head coach of the Texas Longhorns men's basketball team recently requested that Dr. Neff and her research team teach his athletes these practices; and one of the core values of the Golden State Warriors is compassion for both self and others.

So when you are feeling bad and facing challenges—after breaking up with someone, fighting with your friends or parents, receiving a disappointing review or grade, or playing poorly—give yourself the gift of self-compassion. Place your hand on your heart (if you wish), and use these simple phrases: It is really rough when [fill in the blank]. Everyone goes through tough times. In this moment, I offer myself kindness and compassion.

Or if you aren't feelin' these phrases, come up with a couple of go-to phrases that work for you. If you aren't sure what to say, think of what you might say to a friend or teammate, or what a supportive teammate, friend, or coach has said to you. See below for more ideas.

Self-Compassion Phrases

I AM HERE FOR YOU.   I know it sucks.

I WiLL bOUNCe baCK.

EVERYONE MAKES MISTAKES.

S--T HAPPENS.   I am resilient.

It happens to the best.

HANG iN THERE.   PEACE!

I HAVE YOUR BACK.   (as in the practice).

Keep calm and carry on.

What doesn't kill you makes you stronger.

Practicing self-compassion is a very simple way to befriend yourself when you're having a rough time. Although it is enough to simply say reassuring phrases to yourself, the more *sincerely* you can offer yourself the same kindness you would offer a friend the more powerful the practice will be. Amy Baltzell, editor of and contributor to *Mindfulness and Performance*, writes:

> Though there is great benefit from practicing mindfulness—the straightforward practice of present moment focus and acceptance of experience (e.g., learning to maintain attentional focus)—an integration of compassion is essential to learn to tolerate negative emotions and thoughts as they arise. (2016, 60)

Activity: There's a Winner and a…

We can learn a great deal from elite athletes about developing healthy attitudes toward both winning and losing. Consider the comments from Shawn White (two-time snowboard half-pipe gold medalist) after he placed fourth at the 2014 Olympics:

> There is nothing more motivating than actually taking a loss. You get to reflect, you refocus, get inspired, and come back. And that's really the thrill of it, is to come back and see what you've got. [The loss made me] so much better than I was, I think as a person and as a competitor. Having taken that loss, I mean the worst thing I could imagine happened and I was still there. I was still me. (NBC 2016 summer Olympics prime-time broadcast, August 15, 2016)

How would you complete the phrase "There's a winner and a…"?

There's a winner and a _____.

What is the most common way to complete the phrase?

There's a winner and a _____.

Are the way you completed the phrase and the most common way
the same? Circle one: Yes.   No.

When you win, how do you feel emotionally?

_____

_____

When you win, how do you feel in your body?

_____

_____

When you win, how do you feel about the phrase "There's a winner and a loser"?

_____

_____

When you "lose," how do you feel emotionally?

_____

_____

When you "lose," how do you feel in your body?

_____

_____

When you "lose," how do you feel about the phrase "There's a winner and a loser"?

_____

_____

Does the saying "There's a winner and a loser" put you
in the domain of self-esteem or self-compassion?
Circle one: Self-esteem.   Self-compassion.

Are there other more empowering ways to complete the phrase?

There's a winner and a _____.

    Stop. Step outside the invisible, insane cultural boxes of winning or losing. Consider other options.

    Then turn to the next page and read my favorite way to complete this phrase.

There is a winner and a LEARNER.

When you read this, how do you feel emotionally?

_____

_____

How do you feel in your body when you read that phrase?

_____

_____

Does the saying "There's a winner and a learner" put you
in the domain of self-esteem or self-compassion?
Circle one: Self-esteem.   Self-compassion.

When you read this phrase, is there any part of you that says, *Yeah, that's nice, but there are really winners and losers*. To be honest, a part of me says that too. However, the fact that on any given day there are winners and losers, by the stopwatch or the scoreboard, does not mean that on any given day there aren't also learners. The choice is up to you. Win or lose you can *choose* to be a learner.

Every athlete who stands on the podium, kisses a medal, hoists a trophy above her head, or wears a championship ring has also lost hundreds of times. It is what they have chosen to do after the agony of defeat that allowed them to taste the thrill of victory.

So, after every win or loss, make it a practice to write down five things you did well and five things you learned or could improve upon. The following deep reflection from Pat Conroy conveys the true power of choosing to learn in the face of loss:

But losing—there's a deeper music in loss. There really is something about losing that you have to figure out what you did wrong, you have to change the way you played, you have to look at yourself in a different sort of way. Losing seemed to prepare me for life—bad reviews, my mother dying. There was nothing about my mother's death that reminded me anything about winning. (NPR 2016)

Activity: Goals and Intentions

As athletes, and as people, we are often encouraged to set goals. Take a moment and list some of your goals. Then, consider whether your goals fall into the domain of self-esteem (SE) or self-compassion (SC), circling one.

1. _____ SE   SC

2. _____ SE   SC

3. _____ SE   SC

4. _____ SE   SC

Most goals—to make the team, to set the record, to win the championship—depend on external factors beyond our control and specific outcomes. So goals fall into the domain of success or failure, win or lose—that is, the domain of self-esteem. In contrast, intentions are internal, within our control, and describe *process* rather than outcome. Because intentions are about process, they are much less likely to involve success-failure, win-loss, better-worse thinking. Thus, intentions move us beyond the domain of self-esteem, and beyond the need for self-compassion, and into the game.

The following quotes capture the distinction between goals and intentions. Brandi Chastain describes *how* she will play, rather than setting goals regarding specific outcomes, such as number of goals scored. She states that her intentions are to

communicate better with the team; work on the outside of my left foot; make more runs to get into positive positions in the attack; tackle hard and low to keep balance… While winning and losing aren't always in my control, I understand it is up to me to get the most out of my experience on the field. (2004, 132)

Note that her first intention is about team communication, a topic we will return to in the sections "The Magic Ratio and Filling Emotional Tanks" (chapter 14) and "Mindful Communication" (chapters 10 and 14).

In *The Champion's Mind*, Jim Afremow captures the distinction between being driven by ego and goals, rather than mastery and intentions:

Ego-oriented [goal-oriented] student-athletes may be excessively concerned with their stats on the field (e.g., batting average) and GPAs in the classroom. This orientation is associated with higher levels of performance anxiety, as well as discouragement in the face of failures or setbacks, because motivation is mostly contingent on extrinsic [outside] factors, such as others' opinions.

Furthermore, there can be an overwhelming sense of emptiness for ego-oriented athletes after accomplishing their top goal because they are looking in the wrong place to find personal happiness. In contrast, student-athletes who approach tasks with an orientation toward mastery [intentions] are mainly motivated by intrinsic rewards, such as love of the game and pursuit of growth and development. (2013, 92)

Being a competitive athlete means that you probably do many things differently than most people; you devote hours to training, you eat nutritious food, you go to bed early, and so on. This chapter has given you three additional things that you can do differently to help you achieve peak performance and find flow in sports and in life—create a mistake ritual, practice self-compassion, and set intentions.

Giving Yourself the Gift of Mindfulness

We are human; we make mistakes. It is how we *respond* to those mistakes that determines the quality of our relationships—with ourselves and with others. So the next time you make a mistake during practice or competition, use your mistake ritual, have a sense of humor, offer yourself compassion, and return your attention to the present moment. Then, take the time to learn what you can, and set your intentions for upcoming practices and games. Not only will practicing these skills help you master your sport, but developing the ability to compassionately bounce back and learn from mistakes will also help you in school, at work, in relationships, and throughout your life.

Spend the next week or so:

- Choosing or creating a mistake ritual

- Practicing self-compassion

- Being a student of the game and learning from both wins and losses

- Setting intentions

CHAPTER 10

Being a True Teammate

When you're part of a team, you stand up for your teammates. Your loyalty is to them. You protect them through good and bad, because they'd do the same for you.

—Yogi Berra, baseball player, coach, and manager
who appeared in twenty-one World Series

Many of the skills you practiced in earlier chapters can help you improve your relationships with your teammates, and improving your relationships can enhance the team's performance. Applying mindfulness to your interactions with teammates also provides a wonderful opportunity to review much of what we have covered so far. You can also use these same skills to improve your relationships with friends, family members, romantic partners, classmates, roommates, coaches, teachers, colleagues, bosses, and employees. Most people find that when they communicate mindfully they have less drama in their lives and more focus and energy for the things they love.

The following quote from George Yoeman Pocock, shell builder and unofficial spiritual advisor for the 1936 Olympic crew team, also known as "the boys in the boat," expresses the essence of this chapter's message:

[Pocock] suggested that Joe [one of the rowers] think of a well-rowed race as a symphony, and himself as just one player in the orchestra. If one fellow in an orchestra was playing out of tune, or playing at a different tempo, the whole piece would naturally be ruined. That's the way it was with rowing. What mattered more than how hard a man rowed was how well everything he did in the boat harmonized with what the other fellows were doing. And a man couldn't harmonize with his crewmates unless he opened his heart to them. He had to care about his crew. It wasn't just the rowing but his crewmates that he had to give himself up to, even if it meant getting his feelings hurt. (D. J. Brown 2013, 134)

Pocock emphasized to Joe that "if you don't like some fellow in the boat…you have to learn to like him. It has to matter to you whether he wins the race, not just whether you do" (D. J. Brown 2013, 134). Learning to like and work with all your teammates is the essence of being a *true* teammate.

Practice: Filling Your Teammates' Emotional Tanks

In his book *Elevating Your Game*, Jim Thompson describes a simple and meaningful practice of *filling emotional tanks*—offering sincere acknowledgment, encouragement, and support. Filling emotional tanks is even more powerful when done as a mindfulness practice, meaning intentionally with your full, kind, and curious attention.

A beautiful example of timely tank filling comes from the semifinals game of the 2015 women's World Cup. US defender Julie Johnston flicked the ball back to goalkeeper Hope Solo. German midfielder Alexandra Popp intercepted it and drove toward the goal. Johnston pulled Popp down in the box, resulting in a yellow card and a potentially game-changing penalty kick. Seven teammates reassured her that it would be okay, regardless of the outcome of the penalty kick (Litman 2015). At a critical moment, Johnston's teammates used timely tank filling and compassionate communication to support her in getting her head back in the game. Popp failed to score on the penalty kick, and the US went on to win 2–0.

If you are truly committed to becoming a leader, you can engage in *advanced* tank filling. Since you began reading this book you have been practicing bringing your kind and curious attention to physical sensations, thoughts, feelings, reactions, and choices. Now you have the skills to notice, with kindness and curiosity, when you are stingy with support and acknowledgment, when you are just kissing ass, and when you offer *genuine* encouragement and appreciation.

List the teammates to whom you offer encouragement easily and frequently.

_____

_____

List the teammates with whom you are stingy.

_____

_____

List the teammates with whom you are neutral—that is, neither generous nor stingy.

_____

_____

For the next couple of weeks, practice filling emotional tanks. Work your way through the roster, focusing on one teammate, coach, or staff member each day, or each week throughout the season. Filling tanks ensures that you maintain the magic ratio of at least five positive interactions to every negative interaction in your relationships (see chapter 5). Don't forget to fill your own tank through positive scanning (chapter 5) and redefining winning.

As with physical skills, such as dribbling and shooting with your nondominant hand or foot, it is human to have teammates with whom you find it harder and less natural to be generous. And as with physical skills, it is important to work on your "teammate" weaknesses, putting extra effort into filling the tanks of the teammates you tend to neglect or dislike. With kindness and curiosity, simply notice any resistance you have to filling a particular teammate's tank. Usually stinginess and ass-kissing come from jealousy, insecurity, anger, and fear. So can you practice having these feelings without your feelings having you? Can you commit to filling every teammate's tank, especially the teammates you find most difficult?

Sometimes you may need to have a mindful conversation and clear the air before you can find flow with filling the tanks of certain teammates. How to have these conversations will be covered later in this chapter.

Remember, no team can perform at its best when jealousy, insecurity, fear, and anger are burbling under the surface. Pat Summitt, former University of Tennessee women's basketball coach, eight-time NCAA champion, and the winningest basketball coach in NCAA history, wrote that "with attitude, you can determine your own performance. But more than that, you can help determine the performance of others. A single individual with a strong positive attitude can lift those around her. She can change the course of events" (Summitt and Jenkins 1998).

Note to Coaches

The practice of tank filling can be formalized. You can create a simple rotation in which each player is assigned to fill the tank of one other player for one week of the season. Make sure you create a rotation that ensures that each teammate fills every other teammate's tank. For very large teams, such as with football, you may want to create rotations within subteams—offense and defense.

Basic Concept: Reading the Mental and Emotional Game

Many athletes use the concept of reading the game for their sport. Usually it refers to the physical game—Where are your open players? Where are your opponents? Can you anticipate the trajectory of the pass? Can you draw a defender to create space? While it is crucial to read the physical game, it is equally important to read the mental and emotional game. Is a teammate getting agitated and ready to lash out? Is a teammate getting down on himself and checking out? Would it be helpful to offer a kind word, a pat on the back, or a specific suggestion, such as "Shake it off"?

You can take this concept one step further, to reading the game off the ice, court, or field. Maybe you know that a teammate is having a rough time at home or at school, going through a breakup, or dealing with an injury. Perhaps you can let her know that you have her back and are available if she wants to talk or just chill. Better yet, invite her over to hang out or to grab a quick bite to eat. Kobe Bryant, five-time NBA champion and eighteen-time NBA all-star, noted that being a leader and winning a championship involves

> understanding others and what they may be going through… When you understand that, you can communicate with them a little bit better and bring out the best in them. Bringing out the best in people isn't passing them the ball and giving them open shots. It's about how to connect with them, how to communicate with them so that they can navigate through whatever issues they may be facing. That's a very, very hard thing to do. (Holmes 2015)

To feel the power of offering this type of support to a teammate, it can help to write out an example. Below, write a brief description of a time when you were struggling and a teammate reached out to you. Be sure to include what that kindness meant to you.

_____

_____

_____

_____

_____

Basic Concept: Emotional Wave Theory

In chapter 6 you learned basic emotion theory and practiced watching your emotional waves. In life, our emotional waves frequently combine with other people's waves. In fact, in most situations in daily life, such as those that occur on a team, in a group of friends, or in a family, many different emotional waves can combine at one time.

In physics, when two big waves peak at the same time, they create an extremely large, powerful wave, and this is called *constructive interference*. When a big wave meets smooth water, or a big wave combines with a trough, the big wave is neutralized, creating calmer water; this is called *destructive interference*. Sometimes things aren't so simple, and the combination of different waves creates what is known as *mixed interference*.

Here are some very basic visual representations of these wave combinations. In the first two images each line on the left represents the emotions of one person in an interaction, and the line on the right shows the height of the combined wave.

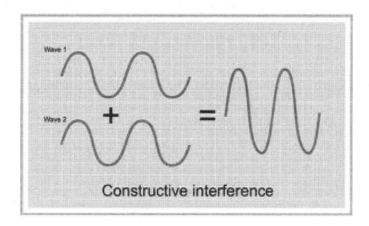

Constructive interference

Can you recall a time when someone, maybe even you, had a big wave and then another person, or several people, added their big waves, and there was a team tsunami? Dramatic examples of team tsunamis are bench-clearing brawls.

_____

_____

_____

_____

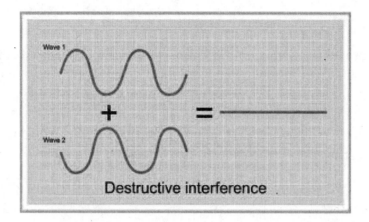

Destructive interference

Can you recall a time when someone, maybe even you, had a big wave, and then another person, or several people, added a calm trough, creating smooth waters? The comments of Julie Johnston's teammates, detailed in an earlier section, are a beautiful demonstration of both emotional tank filling and adding calm rather than upset in a difficult moment.

_____

_____

_____

_____

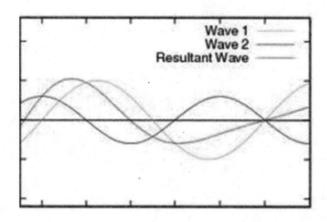

Can you recall a time when someone, maybe even you, had a big wave, and different people added various combinations of big waves and smooth water? One common example of mixed interference in sports is when individual team members react or respond to changes in the coaching staff. Often some people are extremely upset, whereas others try to make the best of it and move forward.

_____

_____

_____

_____

To further complicate things, one person may have more than one emotional wave at a time, and multiple people may be involved in a particular situation. Consider this the next time you're in the middle of a heated moment or disagreement. At a minimum, when we realize we are in an emotional tsunami, we can move to higher ground and allow its intensity to pass.

These examples of emotional waves are not meant to suggest that you will never be upset, or that you will always be able to add calm to a situation. And learning to _respond_ to your emotional waves and the emotional waves of others can literally be a game changer. Consider what might have happened in the 2015 Women's World Cup semifinals against Germany if, after Julie Johnston's error and the resultant opportunity for Germany, all of the US players had been overcome by waves of hopelessness, doubt, or anger. One of the most skillful ways to engage with upsetting situations is to practice mindful communication, as described in the next section.

Activity: Mindful Communication

At times, we will feel extremely angry, sad, disappointed, or frustrated with a teammate, coach, family member, or friend. In the heat of the moment, at the peak of the refractory period, we often react and blurt out serious nastiness. If the person we're interacting with does the same thing, we soon find ourselves tossed about on huge waves of reactivity, drowning in a shared tsunami of toxicity. In both sports and daily life, it is important to find a constructive way to deal with difficulties. To start this activity, take several slow deep breaths, settling into stillness and quietness. Then remember a difficulty you had (or avoided) this week—an issue or discussion with a teammate, coach, friend, family member, teacher, coworker, or someone else. Once you have a clear memory of the interaction, describe it at the top of the worksheet at the end of this activity.

The first step in the process of communicating skillfully is asking yourself, "What did I feel? And what did I want?" Do your absolute best to be real with yourself, and write the answers in the top bubble. It's fine to summarize in just a few brief words or phrases. Sometimes the answers to these questions are quick and clear. At other times, it may be helpful to slow down and _really_ listen to what was true for you. Before moving on to the next step, it's important to acknowledge your _true_ feelings and desires.

The second step is considering what the other person felt and wanted. This is the step we are tempted to skip. Yet without this step, it's often difficult, if not impossible, to communicate and move toward a solution. So, for just a few moments, let go of what you felt and wanted and *really* consider what the other person felt and wanted. When you truly *get* the other person's experience, write a few brief words or phrases describing it in the middle bubble.

Now that you have a better understanding of what both you and the other person felt and wanted, the third step is to consider how you might have gotten out of this hole. What different streets could you have chosen? Are there any creative solutions you overlooked? If you have some ideas, write them in the bottom bubble. If you feel stuck, consider talking to a friend or trusted advisor about possible solutions.

You may think, *Forget this! I don't care.* Yet if you were or are still upset, it's likely that you did or still do actually care. Maybe you just cared about getting what you wanted, which is totally normal. Or maybe you cared about the person you were arguing with. Or maybe, as is often the case, you cared about both.

In difficult interactions, being honest about our own feelings and desires and considering the feelings and desires of others helps us be kinder to ourselves and those we're dealing with. Sometimes we can do this only after the fact, and *sometimes*, if we are really practicing mindfulness, we can slow down and do this process in real time. If things have gotten out of hand in real time, you may need to walk away, cool down, or just take a deep breath and begin again—pausing, moving through the described steps in your head and heart, and then saying something like, "Hey, we got off to a bad start. Can we start over? I'm doing my best to share what's important to me with you, *and* to *hear* what's important to you, so that we can come up with something that works for both of us. Can we slow down and try this again?"

As you continue to practice mindful communication, do your best to not rush the process. Really take the time to understand what's true for you *and* for the other person. For example, if a teammate yelled at you during a game, you might be tempted to pretend you don't care. However, your truth may be *I felt angry and stressed, and I don't play well when he yells at me.* Sometimes, it can seem vulnerable or scary to admit how you really feel and what you really want, even if you're only admitting it to yourself.

You may be surprised by what you discover when you take the time to understand what's really true. You might realize that even though you didn't like your teammate's tone, he was just trying to help, and his comment about your pass or shot was accurate. You might see that he feels insecure and could use some support and tank filling. Or you may find there is a deeper issue that needs to be addressed if the team is going to perform at its best.

Even if you don't like what you discover, acknowledging what you feel and want and what the other person feels and wants provides you with the information you need to consider your choices. For example, if you realize your teammate's comment was accurate, you might say, "You know, you were right about that pass. I am sorry I got pissed at you. And I will play better if you offer specific suggestions in a helpful tone." Or if you realize he is feeling stressed and insecure, you might say, "Hey, it seems like you are having a rough day. Hang in there."

MINDFUL COMMUNICATION

Difficulty: _____

I feel. I want.

The other person feels.
The other person wants.

Possible solutions.

Basic Concept: Acceptance—You Can't Always Get What You Want

Particularly during difficult communications, it is helpful to remember that much as we all wish we could get everything we want in life, the reality is we can't. I can't always get what I want. You can't always get what you want, and others can't always get what they want either. There are definitely times when it's unwise to compromise, and other times when no solution can come close to satisfying everyone. In these situations, it's best to pause and really listen for what's true for you. In certain situations, you may realize that what you thought you wanted isn't what you really want. In other situations, you may find peace by accepting things the way they are. Remember that Suffering = Pain × Resistance.

The less we resist, or the more we accept things as they are, the happier we will be—or at least the wiser we will be. When we know that the roster is set, or that someone will still be a teammate but not a friend, we can take as much time as we need to grieve and heal, and then move forward. Remember, acceptance doesn't mean giving up; it means recognizing that things are the way they are and then discovering your next sane and joyful step. Sometimes we can't change the outside (the circumstances), so the only option we are left with is to change the inside (our thoughts and stories about the situation).

Practice: If You Spot It, You Got It

The phrase "If you spot it, you got it" comes from 12-step programs, and it captures a basic human truth: much of our upset comes from our judgments and stories about people. So in the privacy of this book, knowing that what you write will not be shared with anyone, take a moment to breathe and "sit with" each of your teammates in turn. Slowly bring each teammate into your mind and heart. Then with kindness and curiosity, notice your thoughts and feelings about each one. *Be honest.* The more real you are with yourself, the more you will learn. One or two thoughts and feelings for each teammate is enough. Write them down on the following worksheet.

Again, this is a good place to remember that if your entire team is using this book, you all promised to respect each other's privacy; everyone agreed that if they happened to find someone else's book they would return it without opening it. This is a matter of trust. And trust is an essential element of teamwork. Also, notice if you are tempted to share your thoughts about one teammate with another, or to ask teammates to share their thoughts with you. Then choose integrity—choose to keep your thoughts to yourself, choose not to engage in gossip. You will be glad you did.

IF YOU SPOT IT, YOU GOT IT

Teammate	Thoughts	Feelings

Now pause and breathe. Remember the Nine Dots puzzle and the section "Thinking Outside the Box" from chapter 5? The thoughts and feelings you wrote down for your teammates represent the boxes you put them in. So this week see if you can notice moments when your teammates, particularly those you have difficulty with, behave in ways that are outside the boxes you have created for them—for example, when the "ball hog" actually makes a great pass (this is an opportunity to fill her emotional tank) or your "chill" teammate is a bit snarky. Again, it is helpful to remember that all people (ourselves included) are much more complex than the simplistic boxes we put them in.

Now you can try an extremely advanced, high-degree-of-difficulty mindfulness practice. Take a few deep breaths and settle into stillness and quietness. Then bring your kind and curious attention to your thoughts and feelings about the first teammate on your list. Consider what you wrote for this teammate. Now realize that *whatever* you wrote for that teammate, be it positive, negative, or neutral, you *share* those same qualities. For some of us it may be easier to see that we share the positive qualities. For those of us who feel insecure, we may not believe we share these positive qualities. Most of us don't want to believe we share the negative qualities.

And yet, if we are fearlessly honest we will realize that we have absolutely *every* quality we listed for each teammate. If you think you don't, you are fooling yourself. For example, the thought *He's a ball hog* can only appear when I want the ball. And if I want the ball when I don't have the ball, that makes *me* a ball hog. Mentally I am hogging a ball I don't even have. And if I am *only* thinking *Pass it to me!!!* I am probably missing other crucial elements of the game. Similarly, I can only think *She's so chill* if I am chill enough that I notice her chillness.

Over the next week or month, bravely look at the boxes you put your teammates in and be courageous enough to find the ways you behave similarly. If we are committed, true champions who do this drill full out, we will discover that we have the very habits and behaviors that annoy us the most, those we judge most harshly.

Two athletes from the 2016 Rio Olympics provide contrasting examples of this principle. Although these examples involve competitors rather than teammates, they will help you get the idea. After the US women's soccer team lost to Sweden in the quarterfinals, Hope Solo called the Swedish players "a bunch of cowards" (Wyshynski 2016).

Can you see how her remarks were cowardly?

Conversely, after twenty-six match victories in Olympic beach volleyball, when Kerri Walsh Jennings lost to Brazil in the semifinals, she took responsibility for the loss and praised her opponents, saying, "Tonight, they rose to the occasion" (Wyshynski 2016).

Can you see how she rose to the occasion?

Whatever we spot, and therefore "got," it is helpful to remember we are all doing our best. We are human. We are magnificent. We are flawed. When we can hold these simultaneous truths in our hearts, we can be compassionate with ourselves and others. And if you are finding the *highly advanced* "if you spot it, you got it" practice confusing, or beyond your current abilities, you can work on your fundamentals and come back to it in the future.

Note to Coaches

It can be extremely informative to have your team complete and submit the "if you spot it, you got it" worksheets. It is crucial that you create a structure that allows the players to be completely anonymous, and totally honest. This exercise can reveal invisible patterns and dynamics—for example, unspoken resentments, a quiet player who everyone feels is kind and supportive, or one or two athletes who are gossiping, excluding, or bullying. And if you are willing to up your game, you can include your name and the names of your coaching staff on the forms. You might learn a lot about how your players are responding to your coaching style and your staff.

Basic Concept: Compassion

In chapter 9 you learned about and practiced self-compassion. In my experience, practicing self-compassion helps me be more compassionate with others, and practicing compassion with others helps me be more compassionate with myself. It can be helpful to remember that *just like you*, your teammates have spent hours practicing, want to play well, are human, often feel insecure or jealous, have other stresses (school, work, family, friends), are doing their best, make mistakes, feel terrible when they make mistakes, and on and on.

Being compassionate involves being aware of another's suffering and wishing that the person is relieved of this suffering. A kind word or a small gesture can be a great comfort; you don't necessarily need to *do* anything. Simply being aware of someone's suffering and wishing that they be relieved of that suffering is enough. Compassion is important and meaningful in its own right, and offering compassion often has added benefits. When you acknowledge a teammate's humanity and suffering, it keeps you from judging and criticizing him, and this helps you keep *your* head in the game. When you offer compassion, even if you just silently send kind thoughts, he will likely be less stressed, more present, and better able to play at his highest level. And last but not least, when you practice offering compassion, and your team has compassion as a core value, then you are more likely to receive compassion when you are having a rough time. Ultimately, a culture of compassion allows everyone to feel more at ease and to find flow.

And if you are thinking that compassion is for wimps and that winning athletes are tough and "man up," now is a good time to remind you that compassion is one of the Golden State Warriors' core values. In 2016, assistant coach Luke Walton made the following comments just before the Warriors broke the NBA's longstanding early season consecutive winning streak:

The first one [core value] and the most important one is probably joy…having fun. It's a long season, this game's meant to be fun.

There's mindfulness. There's compassion—for each other and for the game of basketball. And then there's competition.

When we hit those four things, we're not only very tough to beat, but we're very fun to watch, we're very fun to coach, we're very fun to be around. (Kawakami 2015)

Practice: Kindness and Compassion

The concepts of kindness and compassion may seem a bit abstract, and you may be surprised to learn that you can actually practice and develop these skills, just like you practice and develop the physical skills of your sport. These are advanced skills, and it will take time to learn them and understand their value.

So let's practice. Take a quiet moment away from the heat of training and competition to practice offering kindness and compassion to yourself, your teammates, your coaches, and, yes, even the refs and your opponents. While this may sound crazy, I encourage you to give it a try.

Perhaps you can begin very simply, lying in bed at night and repeating the phrases below for yourself and each of your teammates. Begin by resting in stillness and quietness, allowing a feeling of caring, kindness, and love to fill your heart. Often it is easiest to achieve this state by remembering a time when you felt cared for, accepted, understood, and loved. Once you feel some amount (even if it is extremely small) of caring, kindness, or love—or any combination of the three—in your heart, then you can simply say the following phrases in an alternating manner, once for yourself and once for each teammate. It is helpful to begin with teammates that you already feel caring, kindness, and love for, and then, like adding weight during strength training, work your way up to the teammates you find more challenging. You can download an audio recording of this practice at http://www.newharbinger.com/40217.

May I be happy.

May I be focused and responsive.

May I be healthy and free from injury.

May I train and compete with joy and flow.

May Chris be happy.

May Chris be focused and responsive.

May Chris be healthy and free from injury.

May Chris train and compete with joy and flow.

As you repeat the phrases, bring your kind and curious attention to your thoughts, feelings, and physical sensations. It is okay if this feels weird, uncomfortable, or ridiculous. Practicing this advanced skill is like changing your grip on a tennis racquet or the mechanics of your stroke in swimming, and there may be a period of awkwardness before you realize the benefits of this new practice.

As with filling tanks, you will probably find that there are people for whom offering kindness and compassion feels natural and easy, and others for whom it feels more challenging. As with physical training, often the more difficult skills yield the greatest benefits. So stick with the practice and see what happens.

Basic Concept: Generosity

Most of us tend to be self-centered. When we are playing, we're thinking, *Pass to me. I am open.* It is best if we can simply be honest about this human tendency. To counterbalance this common focus on ourselves, we can practice being generous. Successful teams depend on cooperation and generosity. Do you recognize and appreciate your teammates' generosity, which allows you to compete at your best? The loan of a spare pair of socks or prewrap, the kind word, the selfless pass, the constructive feedback, the hours of practice. And then, just like with yoga, can you gently, consistently stretch your heart to be more generous—looking for the open player, offering a compliment, acknowledging the entire team and coaching staff when you are interviewed by the media?

Every successful team depends on generosity and self-sacrifice. One unusual example is road cycling. In cycling it is very common for a rider to sacrifice herself—chasing down a breakaway, pacing the designated climber up the first part of a climb, or leading out a sprint—completely exhausting herself to the point that she does not even finish the race in order to set up a teammate for the win. On healthy teams each rider knows her role and knows that when the opportunity presents itself, her teammates will be generous in return.

Imagine how it would feel to be on a team where everyone practices generosity. And now be the person who creates that reality, that flow.

Activity: Generosity

In order to be generous, we must first acknowledge when we are stingy.

When are you most likely to be stingy?

The list of situations and feelings on the next page are likely to make us feel and act in ways that are stingy. Circle the ones that you know apply to you, and feel free to add others.

Stingy Situations

Nervous   Scouting camps

INSECURE   CHAMPIONSHIPS

PROBLEMS AT SCHOOL

Angry

BIG EXPECTATIONS

TRYOUTS,   Problems at home

PROBLEMS AT WORK

Returning after injury

SELF-DOUBT   Special fans

Remember, we are *all* stingy at times; bringing our kind and curious attention to the situations when we are inclined to be stingy allows us to choose our behavior.

Also, practicing generosity doesn't mean you *always* have to pass and give up the shot. Practicing generosity is simply a way of counterbalancing our human habit of being self-centered and making everything about "I," "me," and "mine."

Basic Concept: Inclusion

Unfortunately, on many teams, from the very youngest youth teams to the NFL, there is a hidden, or in some cases very obvious, culture of relational bullying. *Relational bullying* involves excluding, mean teasing, rumor spreading, secret sharing, alliance building, backstabbing, ignoring, verbal insulting, and hostile body language. As I am sure you realize, these behaviors make it impossible for individual players, and therefore the entire team, to perform at their best.

The "filling your teammates' emotional tanks"; "if you spot it, you got it"; and "kindness and compassion" practices give *you* valuable information about teammates *you* are likely to exclude and be unkind to. More importantly, the practices will support *you* in creating a team culture of inclusion, in which *every* player on the team feels cared for and is therefore able to play his or her best and to find flow. Olympic and World Cup soccer champion Brandi Chastain writes, "You have to find a way to make your relationship with others a positive one, and include everyone in the team environment. The tendency is to gravitate to those we are close to, which is okay, as long as we don't exclude anyone" (2004, 68).

Relational bullying on sports teams is a true epidemic that can have serious long-term negative consequences for all involved—the victim, the bystanders, and even the bully. If this extremely harmful behavior is occurring on your team, it is critical to address it. This topic is covered in more detail in the section "Attending to the Team as a Whole" in chapter 14, and in the "Player Agreement" in the online materials (see http://www.newharbinger.com/40217). Please utilize these resources, share them with your coach and team manager, and, if needed, get additional support from the director of coaching, school, or league officials.

Basic Concept: Beyond Generosity—Making Each Other Better

When we are in flow, we are generous. Or, perhaps more accurately, we move beyond ideas of a separate you and a separate me, beyond generosity and selfishness. We simply *know* or *feel* what is called for in the moment. We are not thinking about ourselves or our teammates— *"She" is open. "I" will pass to her.* Actually, we aren't thinking at all; rather, we're letting the game decide.

In a 2016 press conference, Tony Romo, the long-standing starting quarterback for the Dallas Cowboys, offered an absolutely amazing demonstration of beyond-generous support to his up-and-coming replacement. He had his feelings without his feelings having him, accepted what was, and *chose* to be an extraordinary teammate, when he achingly said that Dak Prescott had

> earned the right to be our quarterback. As hard as that is for me to say he's earned that right…
>
> If you think for a second that I don't want to be out there, than [sic] you've probably never felt the ecstasy of competing and winning… That hasn't left me. In fact, it may burn more now than ever…
>
> I was that kid once. Stepping in and having to prove yourself… But if I remember one thing from back then, it's the people who helped me along when I was young. And if I can be that to Dak, I [will] try to be and can be that person moving forward. (Orr 2016)

Practice: Forgiving Others

Many of us have fixed ideas about what forgiveness is: when, where, and how it should or shouldn't be offered, and who it should and shouldn't be offered to. A simple definition of *forgiveness* is to give up resentment. As athletes, and as human beings, we forgive others for two reasons: first, so that we can work effectively with them on and off the court or playing field, and, second, so that our hearts and minds aren't burdened with judgment, resentment, anger, and hatred. Freeing our hearts and minds helps us be in the moment and find flow.

Forgiving doesn't mean forgetting, or that what happened was okay. It simply means that we recognize that we are all human, that we all make mistakes, and that for our own well-being we *choose* to release the weight of the past and not carry it in the present.

If there is someone who you feel has wronged you or harmed you, rest in stillness and quietness and bring the person, and the harm, to mind. Then fill in the blanks below, and say the sentence silently or out loud to yourself.

[Person's name] _____,

for [specific behaviors] _____

_____ *that have caused me harm, I offer you forgiveness.*

If you have been doing the practices in this book, you probably have developed enough mindfulness that you can simply watch the thoughts and feelings that arise as you practice forgiveness. Notice if you think *F--k this. I am not forgiving him,* if you heart feels hard and closed, or if you feel a subtle sense of ease—a lightening and a softening. Remember that forgiving doesn't mean you have to hang out with the person, room with him, trust him, tell him your secrets, or have any contact with him. It simply means that you acknowledge what happened and are choosing not to let it eat you up inside. The well-known saying "Forgiveness is letting go of all hopes of a better past" embodies this sentiment.

If you are reluctant to forgive, try forgiving for just one minute, five minutes, or for the duration of your next workout, and see how it feels. If, after this brief experiment, you want to pick up and continue carrying your anger and resentment again, that is fine. It may be helpful to remember that you have made mistakes and caused others harm, too. When I acknowledge that I usually cause harm when I am upset, jealous, insecure, angry, afraid, or hurt—physically or emotionally—I find it easier to forgive others.

A passage from *Boys in the Boat: Nine Americans and Their Epic Quest for Gold at the 1936 Berlin Olympics* captures the value of forgiveness, or at least acceptance, for an athlete. In it, Joe, one of the rowers, explains to his wife why he isn't angry with his parents for abandoning him when he was a very young boy. "I just don't understand why you don't get angry," she says. "It takes energy to get angry," he responds. "It eats you up inside. I can't waste my energy like that and expect to get ahead. When they left, it took everything I had in me just to survive. Now I have to stay focused [on rowing]" (D. J. Brown 2013, 134).

As the well-known saying goes, "Holding on to anger is like holding a hot coal with the intention of throwing it at someone else. You are the one who gets burned." It suggests that we practice forgiveness so we don't get "burned." As Joe said, we practice forgiveness so that we don't waste our energy, so that we can stay focused and find flow in sports and in life.

And just one more reminder, forgiveness doesn't mean that the behavior you're forgiving was okay. If a behavior needs to be forgiven, then it was unkind, harmful, or even cruel. Also, just because you forgive someone doesn't mean you don't take steps to address the situation. Have a rigorous, supervised conversation with the person who harmed you; set clear expectations; if necessary, set strict limits on your interactions; and get support from a coach, therapist, institutional governing body, or legal adviser.

Practice: Stretching Toward Sympathetic Joy

The Buddhist practice of sympathetic joy is a unique and wonderful counterbalance to our Western and athletic cultural habits of jealousy, greed, and self-centeredness. *Sympathetic joy* is the practice of taking joy in someone else's joy. Like the generosity practice of an earlier section, sympathetic joy is an advanced practice that you can play with after you have mastered the basics—noticing and befriending disappointment and jealousy, decreasing suffering by decreasing your resistance, and accepting that today was someone else's day, or year, or four years to win (at least in the conventional sense).

Serena Williams demonstrated an extraordinary level of sympathetic joy after she lost to Angelique Kerber at the Australian Open in 2016:

> I was actually really happy for her…
>
> She played so well today. She had an attitude that I think a lot of people can learn from: just to always stay positive and to never give up.
>
> I was really inspired by that. So, honestly…if I couldn't win, I'm happy she did. (Gibbs 2016)

It is important to note that, just like with her tennis skills, it took Williams years to even occasionally attain this level of sympathetic joy. In her younger days she was, by her own admission, a poor loser.

Sympathetic joy is a worthy practice, because ultimately it allows us to transcend our small ego-based selves and discover our expanded hearts. Can you commit to practicing sympathetic joy? Start small. Can you be joyful when your teammate is mentioned in the local newspaper? Can you notice the impulse for jealousy, and then stretch toward feeling joy for this teammate? As with yoga and other physical skills, work at your limit and back off when you need to; this is a skill that will develop over time. Don't pretend or force yourself to be farther along than you are.

Giving Yourself the Gift of Mindfulness

Being a true teammate takes *practice*, and yet the skills for being an excellent teammate are rarely coached. This chapter reviewed fundamental and advanced skills to support you in becoming a true teammate, perhaps even a team leader. These skills are meant to help you notice the human tendencies to be self-centered, reactive, judgmental, stingy, and cliquey and to intentionally balance these tendencies with compassion, generosity, forgiveness, and sympathetic joy. You may want to look back over this chapter and choose one or two concepts or practices to focus on this week, month, or season.

To close this chapter, I will borrow from Jim Afremow, author of *The Champion's Mind*. Please reflect on these three questions regarding your role as a teammate (2013, 23).

1. What am I doing that is hurting my team? [Do I slack off during practice, whine, or talk about my teammates behind their backs?]

_____

_____

_____

2. What am I not doing that is hurting my team? [Do I come prepared and give my best, accept my role on the team, and congratulate teammates on their individual victories?]

_____

_____

_____

3. What are the specific action steps I will take to be a better teammate moving forward? [Hustling on every play, filling my teammate's emotional tanks on and off the playing field or court?]

_____

_____

_____

CHAPTER 11

Almost Moments, Sportsmanship, and Integrity

Sports do not build character. They reveal it.

—John Wooden, ten-time NCAA champion basketball coach

Character is revealed moment by moment in how we respond or react. So let's start with a simple story about responding rather than reacting, shared by a boy in one of my courses. We were discussing unpleasant events, and Michael, a fourth-grader at a low-income school, reported that his new cat had bitten him, that it had hurt, and that he'd wanted to hit the cat. I asked, "Did you?" He smiled and simply said, "No. But I almost did." As a class, we dubbed this an "almost moment." For the remaining five weeks of the course, we explored other almost moments—not hitting the cat at home or the bully on the playground, not giving up on a difficult math problem, not exploding during a disagreement with a friend, and so on—at home, at school, and in life.

As an athlete, you may face more challenging almost moments than most. Examples include choosing how to respond to a ref's bad call, a tough loss, an opponent's taunt, a teammate's "bad idea" or poor behavior; choosing not to cheat to get a better grade; choosing not to use recreational or performance-enhancing drugs; choosing not to have unprotected sex; choosing not to get in the car with a drunk friend; choosing not to join in or allow bullying; or choosing not to participate in or permit the abuse or rape of an incapacitated partygoer.

Every day the pages of newspapers, sports magazines, Facebook, YouTube, and Twitter are filled with examples of athletes revealing poor character on and off the court, such as Lance Armstrong, Marion Jones, and Barry Bonds using performance-enhancing drugs and Ray Rice beating his fiancé in an elevator. To their credit, Jones has expressed sincere remorse, and Rice has committed much of his time to speaking to athletes about preventing domestic violence. Unfortunately, this type of education is much needed. According to the NFL arrest database, 812 players were arrested for assault, battery, domestic violence, drug use, and driving under the influence between 2000 and 2015 (https://www.usatoday.com/sports/nfl/arrests). How different might these athletes' lives, and the lives of those involved, have been if the athletes had learned mindfulness as fourth-graders? What if they had been trained to explore their thoughts and feelings with kindness, curiosity, and perspective, and then to *respond* rather than react in difficult moments? We can never know what would have happened, but perhaps there would have been more smiling postgame interviews and fewer mug shots and court cases. When asked about a particular challenging moment, maybe they would have been able to smile and say, "No. But I almost did."

It is important to realize that your spot on the team, scholarship, career, sponsorship, and postsport opportunities depend on you developing the ability to choose wisely and take a different street in almost moments. *Every time you choose whether or not to drink alcohol or use drugs, or both, is an almost moment.* And drinking alcohol and using drugs definitely increases the risk that you will do things you will regret in the almost moments that follow.

Just ask Ryan Lochte, the Olympic swimmer who, in a series of almost moments, got drunk, vandalized a bathroom, lied about it, subsequently received a ten-month suspension, and then was dropped by his sponsors.

Basic Concept: Respect and Integrity

While there are plenty of examples of athletes making poor choices, fortunately there are many examples of athletes choosing to act with integrity and to honor the game in almost moments. An almost moment in the 2016 Hopman Cup, a tournament leading up to the Australian Open, serves as an example. The ref called a serve from Australian Lleyton Hewitt out. Hewitt conceded the call and went to take his second serve, but his opponent, American Jack Sock, stopped him. "That was in if you want to challenge it," he said. Hewitt was surprised by Sock's admission. When the replay of the serve showed that the ball had indeed been in, the crowd applauded Sock's demonstration of integrity (Scott 2016).

As John Wooden indicates in his statement "Sports do not build character. They reveal it" (Wooden and Reger 2002, 65), we reveal our character in almost moments. When we act with integrity we demonstrate respect for ourselves, our coaches, our teammates, our opponents, the officials, the fans (especially the young ones), and the game. Choosing integrity allows us to have a clear conscience, and having a clear conscience allows us to be in flow and perform at our best. Conversely, when we cheat, our hearts and minds are burdened. Consequently, it is impossible to find flow, and our "victories" are tainted and empty.

Basic Concept: When No One Is Looking

In Michael's class, the discussion of almost moments shifted to a conversation about getting caught—and often punished—when we miss the almost moment, react, and fall into a hole. This led to a discussion about guilt and the experience of feeling guilty, even if we aren't caught. The conversation prompted me to share a well-known story with the group. Because this book is about sports, I have taken the liberty of modifying the original story.

Once upon a time, in the heart of a big city, there was a famous baseball program. One day the coach who ran the program decided to teach his players a lesson. He gathered them and said, "As you can see, I am growing old and slow. I can no longer provide for the needs of the program as I once did. I can think of only one thing that will keep our program from closing. We must win the championship, and for us to do that you must take these pills that will make you stronger and help you hit farther. And no one can know about this. You must take these pills behind the dugout when no one is looking, and *only when no one is looking*. After we win the championship, we will have enough money to continue our famous program."

"But coach," the players said in disbelief, "you have taught us that it is wrong to take anything to enhance our performance. You taught us that it is wrong to cheat."

"Yes, indeed I have," the old coach replied. "It would be wrong, if it were not absolutely necessary. And remember, you must not be seen! If *anyone* can see you, you must not do it! Do you understand?"

The players looked nervously from one to another. Had their beloved coach lost it? "Yes, coach," they said quietly.

"Good," he said. "Now go, and remember, you must not be seen!" The players got up and left the field. The old coach rose slowly and watched them go. When he returned to his seat, he saw that one young man was still standing quietly in the dugout. "Why did you not go with the others?" he asked. "Don't you want to help save our program?"

"I do, Coach," said the player quietly. "But you said that we had to take the pills without being seen. I know that there is no place on earth that I would not be seen, for I would always see myself."

"Excellent!" exclaimed the coach. "That is just the lesson that I hoped you and the others would learn, but you were the only one to see it. Run and tell your teammates, before they get us into trouble." The young man ran and got his teammates, who were nervously gathered just out of sight of the field, trying to decide what to do. When they returned, the coach told them what the young man had said, and they all understood the lesson.

What does this story have to do with holes, almost moments, and choosing our behavior?

_____

_____

_____

In almost moments, when we are headed toward a hole, our mindful awareness always sees. It is quietly watching and will guide us *if* we pause and listen. (For an advanced version of this practice, see "Vigilance and Addictive Mind," chapter 12.)

Practice: THINK! Before Texting or Posting

While we're on the subject of responding and communicating, let's explore mindful texting and posting on social media. Most athletes I know text and post on social media many times each day. While social media is great for staying in touch with friends and sharing your journey, being able to communicate quickly, to more or less the entire world, can sometimes cause problems. The following quote from Justin Stepp, football coach for Southern Methodist University, succinctly sums up the costs of mindless social media posts: "Came across an awful Twitter account today. Shame the kid was a really good player… On to the next…get a clue" (2016). As Coach Stepp's comment indicates, it's always wise to THINK before you text, post, or speak.

Before you speak:

THINK!

T — is it true?

H — is it helpful?

I — is it inspiring?

N — is it necessary?

K — is it kind?

I like to add an exclamation point to THINK! It is there to encourage you to pause and consider a couple of additional questions before posting:

- Would you want a friend or teammate to post a similar comment, photo, or video about you?

- Would you feel good about your mother, grandma, little brother or sister, teammate, coach, scout, or sponsor seeing your comment, photo, or video?

Using the THINK! practice before speaking, texting, or posting can prevent you from putting words and images out into the world that you will later regret.

Lindsey Vonn, legendary US downhill ski racer, learned this lesson the hard way. Her impulsive behavior, combined with impulsive posting of videos of her behavior, almost cost her a very lucrative ten-year ski and binding sponsorship. During a World Cup event, Vonn went wide on a turn and put all her weight on the inside of her left ski. The right ski detached as it hit a bump. Vonn fell and slid down the course on her hip; she was bruised but otherwise uninjured. Her sponsors were definitely *not* pleased when she publicly blamed equipment failure for her fall, destroyed her bindings with a hammer, and *then* posted a video of her outburst on her social media feeds (Dampf, no date). (We will return to this story in the section on mistakes and amends.)

Prospective coaches want to see posts that show love and respect for family, high school coaches, and teachers, posts that indicate "the recruit isn't 'too cool' to interact with the people who provide so much for them" and that "show a level of gratitude" (Samuels 2016). Take a moment and list five types of posts that might impress coaches and scouts. Don't quit until you get to five. If you are struggling, look at the section titles of the next chapter, "Habits of Excellence."

1. _____

2. _____

3. _____

4. _____

5. _____

Reflection: THINK! About the Comments of Others

In a recent session with a young athlete, I pointed out that the THINK acronym can also help us choose how we respond to others' thoughts, comments, texts, and so forth. When someone—a teammate, an opponent, a family member, a fan, a reporter—comments on you, your abilities, or your behavior, you may want to pause and ask the following:

- Is it true? (Remember, the more our personalities don't like or are offened by feedback, the more likely it is true.)

- Is it helpful? (If we are willing to hear it, rigorous feedback can be extremely helpful.)

- Is it inspiring?

- Is it necessary?

- Is it kind?

If you can't answer yes to at least three of the five questions above, then you can simply let the statement go. Multi-record-setting MLB player Shawn Green offers this wise reflection about responding to the comments and critique of others:

Finding stillness…enabled me to understand the pitfalls of allowing the ever-changing external world to dictate my inner world. If one stranger's opinion could actually change my stress level, anger level, and overall well-being, then who was actually at the controls of my life? (2011, 22)

Basic Concept: Mistakes, Apologies, and Amends

Even if we are practicing mindfulness, we are human. And in our humanness, when we are overcome by fear, anger, disappointment, or jealousy, we sometimes screw up and say or do something we regret. Then the best that we can do is acknowledge the mistake, take responsibility for it, apologize, and make amends.

Interestingly, while gold medal sports performances are rare, gold medal apologies are even harder to find. Let's return to Lindsey Vonn; with her sponsorship at risk, and with the help of her agent, she issued the following apology for uploading the video of herself destroying her ski bindings:

This was a huge mistake born out of the frustrating race I had today and was in no way, shape or form a reflection on the performance of the Head race team and the Head skis and bindings which I race on, and which have been instrumental in my success. In fact, thank goodness the binding released as it should, preventing a possible injury…

I'm disappointed in myself… I should know better and I do know better and I just let my emotions get the best of me and I didn't think [THINK!] it through. Social media is a great platform if it's used correctly and in that case it was not used correctly and I apologize for that and I will not make that mistake again. (Dampf, no date)

A gold medal example of making an apology and *living* amends comes from Indiana Pacers' center Roy Hibbert. His statement and *actions*, after making homophobic comments, demonstrate sincere remorse and true learning:

> I am apologizing for insensitive remarks made during the postgame press conference after our victory over Miami Saturday night. They were disrespectful and offensive and not a reflection of my personal views. I used a slang term that is not appropriate in any setting, private or public… I apologize to those who I have offended, to our fans and to the Pacers' organization. I sincerely have deep regret over my choice of words last night. (Buzinski 2013)

In terms of *living* his amends, Hibbert subsequently went on to express support for Jason Collins when he came out as the first openly gay NBA player.

Practice: Apology

Offering a sincere apology and making true amends takes practice. "Accountability is essential to personal growth, as well as team growth," wrote Pat Summitt, University of Tennessee women's basketball coach, eight-time NCAA champion, and winningest basketball coach in NCAA history. "How can you improve if you're never wrong? If you don't admit a mistake and take responsibility for it, you're bound to make the same one again" (Summitt and Jenkins 1998). Pause here for a moment and consider what you feel are the essential qualities of a sincere and heartfelt apology.

Before you look at the next page for suggestions, write your ideas in the space below.

_____

_____

_____

_____

_____

_____

Apology Practice

Below are the essential elements of a true, heartfelt, and meaningful apology:

1. Take time to *really* understand and *feel* how your action, or inaction, caused harm.

2. Apologize in person, *only* if apologizing will not cause further harm.

3. Apologize in a timely manner, preferably before, or at the very least immediately after, your mistake becomes public. There are endless examples of athletes who initially make up elaborate stories, blame others, and claim they are not guilty, and only after the facts come to light do they acknowledge their mistakes and offer an apology.

4. Apologize sincerely: Take responsibility. Say "I am sorry" with no ifs, ands, or buts.

5. Be specific: Say *how* what you said or did was harmful, wrong, or disrespectful, or how it dishonored the game.

6. Express remorse.

7. Make amends. Do everything you can to make it right.

8. Do better: The statement "When we know better, we do better," attributed to the author Maya Angelou, demonstrates that when we acknowledge and learn from our mistakes, we can do better.

Now it is time for you to practice. Think back, maybe through this week, maybe waaaay back. Do you have anyone you need to apologize and make amends to?

Circle one: Yes. No.

Any time you make a mistake, you can jump-start the apology-and-amends process by completing the prompts below.

I am truly sorry that I _____.

I know I harmed, hurt, offended, and disappointed _____.

What I did was wrong because _____

_____.

I will make it right by _____.

In the future, I will _____.

Practice: Forgiving Yourself and Asking for Forgiveness

In chapter 9 you created a mistake ritual to use when you make errors during training and competition. Apologizing and making amends are the equivalent of a mistake ritual for when we have been unkind and caused harm to another. Once you have acknowledged your mistake, taken responsibility, learned your lesson, apologized, and truly done your absolute best to make amends, then it is time to forgive yourself and move on.

As you learned in the section "Forgiving Others," forgiveness is a skill that you can practice. Forgiving ourselves doesn't mean forgetting, or that what we did was okay. To repeat, if a particular action deserves or requires forgiveness, then the action was unkind, harmful, or cruel. Offering forgiveness to ourselves and others simply means that we recognize that we are all human, that we all make mistakes, that we can choose to take responsibility (notice that "respond" and "responsibility" have the same root) and learn from our mistakes. Practicing forgiveness allows us to find flow in sports and in life.

If after you have done your rigorous soul-searching, apologized, and made amends you find that you are still beating yourself up, you can breathe, rest in stillness and quietness, and repeat this phrase:

I offer myself forgiveness for the things I thought, said, and did that caused people harm.

Be as specific as possible about what you thought, said, and *did*, and to whom:

I offer myself forgiveness for trash-talking Nick and Tom.

Now check in with yourself. Perhaps simply beginning to forgive yourself feels like enough for today. However, if you are feeling brave and willing, you can step it up a notch and silently say to yourself:

Nick and Tom, I ask for your forgiveness for trash-talking you.

Just notice the thoughts and feelings that arise as you try this.

Remember, there is no need to ask for forgiveness in person. If you want to go for the gold, you can ask the people you harmed for forgiveness in person. If you do that, it's important to keep in mind that it doesn't matter how they respond. You may be surprised at how freeing it is to simply acknowledge any harm you caused and humbly ask for forgiveness. Believe me, I know.

Giving Yourself the Gift of Mindfulness

As with physical skills, forgiveness and the more advanced mental, emotional, spiritual, and relational skills in this chapter and the following chapters have a progression. Like the progression in gymnastics of tucked backflip, piked backflip, laid-out backflip, and double-tucked backflip, forgiving yourself, silently asking for forgiveness, and asking for forgiveness in person are progressive steps building toward the complex processes that are required to be a truly amazing teammate, friend, roommate, brother, sister, daughter, son, girlfriend, boyfriend, wife, husband, boss, employee, and so on.

For the next week or so practice the following:

- Choose wisely in your almost moments.

- THINK! before you speak, post, or act.

Practicing these skills will definitely decrease the number of times you will need to practice

- offering a sincere, detailed apology;

- making amends;

- forgiving yourself; and

- asking for forgiveness.

CHAPTER 12

Habits of Excellence

We are what we repeatedly do. Excellence then is not an act, but a habit.

—Aristotle

As noted in previous chapters, facing challenges, taking responsibility for mistakes, and responding in almost moments help us develop habits of excellence. In this chapter, we will briefly revisit some habits of excellence that were touched on previously and explore others not yet covered. Each habit can be its own mindfulness practice. For example, you might want to devote a week or a month to practicing gratitude, responsibility, preparedness, finishing, joy, fluidity, sportsmanship, freedom, vigilance, humility, and service. As with physical skills, there are progressions for many of these advanced mental, emotional, and spiritual skills. The previous chapters provided you with solid fundamentals, and now it is time to take your skills to the next level.

Practice: Gratitude

It is human nature to focus on the negative, such as *I didn't stick the landing. She should have passed to me; I was open. I should be getting more playing time.* When you find yourself caught up in negative internal dialogue, it can be helpful to return to the practices of acceptance (versus resistance) and positive scanning; together these practices establish a solid foundation for more advanced gratitude practice. Practicing gratitude brings our focus into the moment and frees our mind from negative internal chatter. Examples of gratitude in action include *I hit the whole routine except the landing. Passing back was a good idea. I am getting playing time.*

True gratitude represents a level of mental, emotional, and spiritual mastery. Using a snowboarding analogy, acceptance is like riding a gentle intermediate run, positive scanning is like working basics in a small half-pipe, and true gratitude is like a competition run in the pipe. True gratitude represents a heartfelt—as in you can actually feel it in your heart—appreciation for your circumstances. *It is a privilege to be on the team. I am so grateful the injury wasn't more serious.* And just like with physical skills, sometimes it takes us *years* of practice to develop these "high degree of difficulty" habits of excellence. So I encourage you to practice acceptance and positive scanning and to work toward hitting true gratitude with increasing consistency, even when conditions are less than ideal.

Each day after practice, or every night before you go to sleep, you can acknowledge five things you are *truly* grateful for. Experiment with being grateful for little things, big things, and things you take for granted. Examples include food, shelter, water, general health (even if you are injured), teammates, coaches, parents, siblings, training facilities, opportunities, opponents (without whom you could not compete), officials, spectators, trainers, bus drivers, janitors, clothing, equipment, and on and on. Take a lesson from Brandi Chastain, Olympic and World Cup soccer champion: "I never want to lose sight of what this game has given me. I want to bask in this gratitude, and let that appreciation always remain alive in me" (2004, 190).

Activity: Responsibility—No Excuses

So often when things don't go our way we make excuses, or blame others. Unfortunately, this habit leaves us hanging, focused on things that are out of our control. We may say things like "I had an off day" or "The coach always chooses his favorites." While these statements may or may not be true, they don't reflect a commitment to taking full responsibility for our performance. And taking full responsibility for our performance is what allows us to learn, improve, and choose our next sane and joyful step. When you look back, what might you have done differently to have prevented yourself from feeling off? Eaten a highly nutritious, more easily digestible lunch, or not walked around the mall between events? And if the truth is that the coach chooses favorites, what skills and qualities do the favorites have that you want to develop?

What are your three most common excuses?

1. _____

2. _____

3. _____

For each excuse above, list at least one specific action that you can take to respond to and take responsibility for the situation.

1. _____

2. _____

3. _____

Basic Concept: Preparedness and Flexibility— Expect the Unexpected

Do your best to avoid snafus when possible. The word "snafu" is derived from a military acronym meaning "situation normal: all f----d up." To minimize the likelihood of snafus, control what you can control. If you are booking your travel, plan to arrive several days before your competition. Make a competition packing list, and triple-check it before you leave. Bring both your home and away uniforms. If you compete outdoors, be prepared for a variety of weather conditions. Have the necessary layers, including clothing for warming up and staying warm after. Always carry food that you know works well for you, such as a couple of high-quality energy bars or trail mix. You never know when your plane will be late and all the restaurants in the airport will be closed, or when you will get stuck in traffic and not have time for lunch. Check the event schedule for changes in start times. Double-check driving directions, and add a generous time cushion to your estimated driving time. Practice in less-than-optimal conditions—poor surface, hot and cold temperatures, noisy environments. Learn to be at your best even when the circumstances are not ideal.

As an example of preparing for less-than-ideal circumstances, my friend Kristen Smyth, head coach of the Stanford women's gymnastics team, has the men's crew team yell at her athletes during their routines. It is quite something to see and hear very large men yelling at petite women practicing beam routines. And you better believe that these young women know how to maintain their composure when their competitors' fans suddenly erupt in cheers.

As another example, consider Francesca, a young national-level diver I have worked with since 2014. She beautifully demonstrated the essence of mindfulness, preparedness, and flexibility during the 2016 Junior National Synchronized Diving Championships, where she competed with two different partners in three events for a total of sixty-four dives over three days of competition! This is even more impressive when you realize that her two partners have two different body types, heights, weights, diving styles, and rotational speeds. These differences required Francesca to be truly focused and in sync with each partner. In a midcompetition email her mother shared this:

Mindfulness practice came in particularly handy this afternoon when we found out, as we were leaving for finals, that Francesca's grandfather had died this morning. Francesca was quite shaken. We talked about it a bit, then laid down and did rest (practice) together. It helped her settle and focus… Thank you for all the tools you have given her.

At age thirteen, Francesca chose to *rest* and *have her feelings without her feelings having her*, and then continue to compete. She went on to become the junior national synchronized diving champion on both platform and 3 meter. Perhaps knowing this will inspire you to step up your mindfulness practice so you develop similar composure and resilience. Please don't overgeneralize this example, or mistakenly interpret it to mean that in the face of tragedy you "should" do some mindfulness and "should" continue to compete. Rather, the invitation is to rest in stillness and quietness, befriend your feelings, and then honor your inner wisdom about what is truly best for you and all involved.

Remember, even when you have done your absolute best to fully prepare for competition, snafus inevitably happen; when they do, you can kindly and gently return to your skills for facing challenges—humor, flexibility, equanimity, faith.

What is the snafu you worry about most?

_____

_____

Can you imagine it, or re-create it, so you can learn to perform well in the most difficult circumstances?

Basic Concept: Finishing—It's Not Over Until It Is Over

Athletic culture is full of sayings, such as "Play until the whistle blows," that emphasize the skill of finishing. And there are hundreds of examples of likely winners celebrating prematurely only to be caught out on the final decisive play or passed at the line. One well-known example happened at the 2006 Winter Olympics in Turin. Lindsey Jacobellis, seven-time X Games snowboardcross champion, had built what should have been an insurmountable lead in the women's final. As she flew down the finishing straight she began hotdogging and did a playful jump and board grab. Then she caught an edge and fell, allowing Switzerland's Tanja Frieden to pass her and take the gold medal. (We will return to Jacobellis's story in the following section on joy.)

It is wise to remember that for each story of premature celebration, there is another competitor—or team—who stayed focused and competed to the line, or until the final whistle, and earned the win. And there are stories like that of Olympic runners Abbey D'Agostino of the United States and Nikki Hamblin of New Zealand, who collided in the 5,000-meter semifinals at the 2016 Summer Olympics in Rio, and then chose to help each other up and finish together with dignity. In fact, D'Agostino finished, despite tearing her ACL and straining her MCL.

And finally, I invite you to imagine a wonderful example of finishing that I recently saw in a video. At the start of a very ordinary eight-and-under girls' 25-meter freestyle swimming race, which could have occurred at any local rinky-dink pool, one young girl slipped and belly flopped onto the starting block; she was splayed out like a squashed bug. Then, she slithered into the pool, many body lengths behind her competition, and determinedly dog-paddled to second place.

Are you willing to commit to the practice of finishing?

Activity: Joy—A Powerful Source of Flow

Let's return briefly to Lindsey Jacobellis. Before you judge her too harshly, remember that we are all human, and we all make mistakes. It is just that most of us aren't competing on the world stage, where our mistakes are literally broadcast to the entire planet. Ironically, Jacobellis didn't win gold, in part, because she was displaying another habit of excellence—joy. After placing second, she said, "I didn't even think twice. I was having fun, and that's what snowboarding is. I was ahead. I wanted to share with the crowd my enthusiasm. I messed up. It happens" (Riley and Dillman 2014). Her comments demonstrate four habits of excellence: joy; acceptance (that is, lack of resistance); willingness to acknowledge, learn from, and let go of mistakes; and self-forgiveness. It may inspire you to know that Jacobellis continues to compete, to embody joy, and to inspire her fellow competitors.

Simone Biles, Olympic all-around champion, inspired her teammates with the power of joy. After one meet, Simone was told that she was getting distracted and enjoying herself too much. She responded, "That was me in my zone… I think I'm teaching my teammates that they can still be successful while having fun, and enjoying the moment rather than being a stone cold brick. You can have fun and do well. Just let loose a bit" (Park 2016).

So how can you bring a quality of joy to your training and competition? And how can you share it with your fellow competitors and fans? Maybe you and your teammates can create a pregame cheer, a playful mistake ritual, or a simple postscoring celebration. This quote from Boris Becker, former number-one tennis player in the world and winner of six Grand Slam titles, will help you keep in mind what is most important about sports: "I love winning. I can take losing. But most of all I love to play."

List one simple way you can bring joy to:

Training: _____

_____

Competition: _____

_____

Daily life: _____

_____

Activity: Fluidity—Moving Along Continuums

Together the two previous sections demonstrate the principle of fluidity.

Most traits exist along a continuum. Notice your thoughts and feelings as you read the following word pair: discipline-playfulness. Do you think and feel that one word is better than the other? The reality is that both qualities are valuable, and with mindfulness we can slide along the continuum, choosing the most useful response in the moment. This is *fluidity*. Can you recognize moments when it would be helpful to be more disciplined? More playful?

Fluidity applies to all human traits, including selfish-selfless, extroverted-introverted, follower-leader. So it is helpful to know your general tendencies. Do you tend to be a selfish, introverted follower? Are there times when it might be beneficial for you to slide along one or more of these continuums?

With kindness and curiosity, mark your default position along the continuums listed below. Please note that in sports and in life there are times and places for each quality.

Disciplined ——————————————————————— Playful

Generous ——————————————————————— Stingy

Extroverted ——————————————————————— Introverted

Follower ——————————————————————— Leader

As mentioned previously, true mindfulness means that we slide freely along multiple continua as needed in the moment.

Basic Concept: Sportsmanship—It Is About More Than the Game

Sportsmanship is another quality that occasionally prompts athletes to choose not to finish—and in some cases to not even start. Consider this story of sportsmanship involving a young wrestler named Amed Castro-Chavez from Estherville-Lincoln Central High School in Spencer, Iowa. Rather than step onto the mat and win by forfeit, he chose to honor Austin Roberts, the young man he should have been wrestling that day. Sadly, Roberts had died wrestling the week before. To honor his fellow competitor, and the grief of Roberts's parents, teammates, coach, and community, Castro-Chavez walked to the bleachers, hugged Roberts's mother, and said he wished he "could wrestle Austin again, because he was such a great wrestler... It was an honor to wrestle Austin" (Gallagher 2016). That, my friends, is true sportsmanship, and definitely a win.

Basic Concept: Freedom—Also Known as Nonattachment

In sports and in life, it's very easy to become overly focused on winning. This, of course, can affect how we perform—and not necessarily in a good way. When we recognize we are obsessing about winning, we can benefit from letting go of outcome and, as sports psychologist Jim Afremow writes, from focusing "on the process and execution rather than worrying about the desired, or worse, the feared result" (2013, 223).

On May 28, 2017, the Golden State Warriors and Oklahoma City Thunder were suiting up for game six of the 2016 Western Conference Series. The series winner (the first team to win four out of the seven games) would go on to play in the NBA Finals. The Warriors trailed the Thunder two games to three. If the Warriors lost game six, they'd lose the series and fail to advance to the finals. The stories in the press and locker room shared common themes: make or break, do or die, win or go home. Because the Warriors' core values are joy, mindfulness, compassion, and competition, I hoped the team would win the series and the NBA championship. And I was extremely curious about how the team was applying these principles, at that particular moment, in the locker room. Although it's presumptuous, this got me thinking, if I could have been in the locker room with them, what would I have said?

Well, for the record, this is what I would have said.

Close your eyes. Rest your attention on your breath. Allow yourself to settle into stillness and quietness. Now simply acknowledge your primary fear in this moment. It is probably something like *We'll lose*. Just be with that. Feel it. Really feel it, in your body, in your mind, and in your heart.

Now what if I told you that it was absolutely guaranteed that you will lose? Step into that reality. At the end of the evening you are going to walk off the court, and this miraculous record-breaking season is going to come to an abrupt end. You won't be playing in the championship series. This is guaranteed.

Breathe. Allow your thoughts and feelings. Watch the *Yes, but…* and the *What the F--K kind of pep talk is this?* thoughts, and let them pass.

Knowing that you will lose, how do you want play? What do you want to remember? What do you want to be able to say when you walk off the court?

Do you want to *know* that you gave it your all? That you played full out, motivated by love of the game, rather than a fear of losing or a desperation to win? Do you want to know that you fully expressed your core values of joy, mindfulness, compassion, and competition?

There is tremendous freedom in facing our fears, letting go of outcomes, and truly *choosing* to play with JOY! In this moment, what are you going to choose?

Now, I assume that after this invitation to reflect on their attachment to winning and the related fear of losing, these determined athletes would still want to win. That's the nature of highly competitive athletes. The intention of this imaginary practice was to encourage the players to watch their thoughts, to befriend their feelings (chapter 6), to loosen the often paralyzing attachment to outcome, and to ultimately find flow. Usually the less you are attached to outcome, the freer you are, and the freer you are the better you compete. Andre Agassi, former number-one tennis player in the world and eight-time Grand Slam winner, noted the benefits of nonattachment in his autobiography *Open*: "Freed from thoughts of winning, I instantly play better. I stop thinking, start feeling. My shots become a half-second quicker, my decisions become the product of instinct rather than logic" (2009, 365).

Basic Concept: Vigilance and Addictive Mind

While freedom and nonattachment support flow, attachment, particularly attachment to winning, can quickly morph into Addictive Mind. I would be remiss if I failed to warn you, as Coach G warned me, that as athletes, as human beings in pursuit of excellence, we will be seduced by an aspect of ego known as Addictive Mind. Even if we have the guidance of a masterful coach and vigilantly practice mindfulness, Addictive Mind can lead us down twisted dark alleyways of thought—thoughts about winning…*winning at all costs*. The following thoughts are sure signposts that we have followed Addictive Mind into seedy neighborhoods: *I have to win. I got here on my own. I don't need my coach. The rules don't apply to me.* Another obvious marker that we have lost our way is an incessant craving for *more*—more winning, more fame, more money, more highs, more sex, and, in some cases, more escape, or more numbness, more… Interestingly, thoughts of extreme detachment can also indicate that we have followed Addictive Mind into dangerous territory. Thoughts of extreme detachment include *It doesn't matter, I don't deserve to be here, I've let everyone down,* and *I'm a loser.* In cases of both extreme attachment and detachment we become so captivated by Addictive Mind's exaggerations, distortions, and lies that we follow it blindly and fail to notice the blatant warning signs. In these states, there is no love of the game, no flow.

From day one, and for the last twenty-eight years, Coach G has said, "It is not when a player is beginning, being introduced to the game, learning the skills, and doing the day-in-day-out hard work—those aren't the tough passages. The most challenging territory is when a player experiences a *succession* of winning. This is the way of *it*, the seduction of Additive Mind." Simply put, we are most susceptible to Addictive Mind when we experience extraordinary success.

Phil Jackson, former coach of the championship-winning Chicago Bulls and Los Angeles Lakers, describes the costs of Addictive Mind as follows: "An obsession with superstardom strokes the ego…and plays havoc with the very thing that attracts most people to basketball in the first place: the inherent beauty of the game" (2014, 5). What is true for basketball is true for all sports. Some examples of exceptional athletes who have been captured by Addictive Mind and completely lost their way are Lance Armstrong, who doped his way to multiple Tour de France titles; players on the 2009–2013 New Orleans Saints, who intentionally injured opposing players for bounties; Tiger Woods, with his extramarital dalliances; Rosie Ruiz, who only ran the last portions of the Boston and New York City Marathons; Tonya Harding, who arranged to have her primary opponent (Nancy Kerrigan) attacked before the 1994 US Figure Skating Championships and Olympic trials; and members of the 1919 Chicago White Sox World Series team, who threw the game for money. In succumbing to Additive Mind, these people cheated, lied, and betrayed teammates, friends, family, and the game.

Although Coach G *repeatedly* warned me about the seductions of Addictive Mind, I too have succumbed to it at pivotal points in my journey. In my case, Addictive Mind defined "winning at all costs" as ruthlessly competing against and beating my beloved coach. It did everything in its power to get me to diminish, negate, erase, and destroy Coach G physically, mentally, emotionally, professionally, legally, and financially. Most recently, in the process of writing this book, Addictive Mind became obsessed with an author's version of "Olympic gold"—that is, writing a best seller. As a result, I again failed to give Coach G credit and arrogantly pretended that I got here on my own. I stole from, lied to, cheated, and betrayed the woman who truly taught me *everything* in this book. This caused Coach G great harm and distress.

Astonishingly, each and every time Addictive Mind seduced me into entering the darkest alleyways, Coach G guided me through the process of repair, amends, restitution, and rebuilding. This is the benefit of sticking with one truly masterful coach: She understands the historical, cultural, and familial addictions to, and simultaneous fear of, winning, success, fame, and fortune. She knows the signature weaknesses, tendencies, habits, and impulses of my particular variation of Addictive Mind. She doesn't take any of it personally. She won't allow me to let myself get away with anything. She devotedly stands for and fights for my strengths, potential, and gifts. Especially when Addictive Mind resists mightily, she always, and in *all ways*, coaches me to bring my best game, and to find flow.

Her fierce, constant, and loving persistence supports me as I humbly remember and *apply* all the lessons in this book: observing seductive ego thoughts, both self-promoting (*My book rocks. I'm The Best, The Expert, The Coach.*) and self-defeating (*F--k this! I can't do it. It's too hard. I quit.*), without believing them or taking them personally; having intense delusions of grandeur and overwhelming feelings of doubt and shame without them having me; choosing, again and again, to do the work, run the drills, and practice the skills; trusting everything (including protracted Addictive Mind episodes) is happening for me, not to me; practicing forgiveness and self-compassion; learning from abject failure; making amends; and, ultimately, realizing that I am not Addictive Mind.

Signposts of Addictive Mind

I Me MINE   Yes, but thinking

More   WANTING

JUSTIFYING   BLAMING

Fear

DEFENDING   Ambition

Lack of joy   Jealousy   Impatience

Viscious Competion   INSECURITY

Arrogance   ABSENCE OF LAUGHTER

Numbness   Shutdown feeling

Crossed-arms f--k-you posture

When I discover that I have lost my way, or, as is more often the case, coach G lets me know, I stop, get out the GPS (Georgina Positioning System), make a legal U-turn when possible, and retrace my steps. This retracing of steps, one distorted thought at a time, is an elite version of the "choosing a different street" activity offered in chapter 7. Dedicated athletes who have surrendered to skillful coaching and courageously retraced their steps include Andre Agassi, who worked his way out of self-loathing; Maria Sharapova, who returned to tennis after taking responsibility for using a banned substance; Abby Wambach and Michael Phelps, who found their way through overwhelming expectations, depression, and alcoholism.

In his book *The Way of Baseball: Finding Stillness at 95 MPH*, multi-record-setting MLB player Shawn Green humbly reflects on his experience of getting lost in ego (Addictive Mind) during periods of success, failure, and injury:

> Was my immoderate labeling of the ego [Addictive Mind] as an evil enemy where I'd gone wrong? After all, the problem is not the ego [Addictive Mind] itself, which is almost impossible to permanently quash, but getting lost in the ego [Addictive Mind] and falsely identifying it as one's own true essence. Might simply being aware of the ego [Addictive Mind] and watching it from a place of separation and space be enough to keep oneself present? (2011, 160)

Like Green, I am learning that the more I am able to be vigilant and simultaneously have compassion for Addictive Mind (ego), the more I am able to stay in the game, play at the highest level, and find flow. Perhaps a fresh sports analogy will clarify this. With both physical habits and Addictive-Mind habits, I have found that it is extremely helpful to *own* that I have particular weaknesses—such as a tendency to overcommit on *defense*. On the court, or the field, when a player overcommits on defense, he is poorly positioned, off-balance, and unable to respond effectively to his opponents. In life, when I overcommit to defending Addictive Mind, I too am flat-footed, rigid, and unable to respond gracefully in the moment. Yet, when I simply acknowledge these addictive habits, I can choose to take a deep breath, a step back, and a more flexible, fluid, and responsive stance; I can choose to open my heart. And it is only by acknowledging, with kindness and curiosity, the dark tendencies of Addictive Mind that I can return to, as Shawn Green says, my essence and let the natural light of self-compassion, forgiveness, compassion for others, generosity, joy, and love of the game shine through.

By reading this book you too are learning to recognize the fantasies and fears of Addictive Mind that will tempt you into seedy neighborhoods, as well as the physical, mental, and emotional signposts that indicate when you have lost your way. You are developing the skills to retrace your steps and return to your essence, to flow, to the love of the game, and, as Coach Dabo Swinney says, to light. To paraphrase Swinney, coach of the 2017 NCAA champion Clemson Tigers, let the light inside you be bigger than the light upon you.

Activity: Humility—No One Does It Alone

Often in sports, and in life, when we have a string of "successes" we can get overconfident, cocky, and arrogant. When Addictive Mind convinces us that we accomplished it all on our own, we can get sloppy and cut corners and can forget that what goes up comes down. So to minimize the likelihood that we will be seduced by Addictive Mind, and to maximize the probability that we will find flow, it is important to remember four principles: (1) the idea of success lives in the domain of self-esteem (versus self-compassion), (2) success is impermanent, (3) success is always a team effort (even for those participating in individual sports), and (4) success is dependent on continuing to practice the physical, mental, emotional, and spiritual fundamentals. Remembering these principles will keep us humble, and humility enhances the probability that we will experience flow.

Daniel Brown beautifully captures the power of humility in *The Boys in the Boat*, a story about eight hardscrabble young men who ultimately won Olympic gold in rowing in 1936:

> They were all skilled, they were all tough, they were all fiercely determined… Every one of them had come from humble origins or been humbled by the ravages of the hard times in which they had grown up… The challenges they had faced together had taught them humility—the need to subsume their individual egos for the sake of the boat as a whole—and humility was the common gateway through which they were able now to come together and begin to do what they had not been able to do before. (2013, 243)

By subsuming our egos to the larger team or game, we allow ourselves to be and do what we have not been and done before.

Humility and gratitude may come more easily and naturally for athletes participating in team sports, but it is equally important for athletes who participate in individual sports to remain humble, to acknowledge that they are also generously supported by a team. The truth is, none of us achieves "on our own," and "our" accomplishments are the result of the kindness, wisdom, encouragement, and support of many people.

After winning the season-long 2015 Tour Championship, and receiving a $10 million bonus, Jordan Speith captured a true champion's combination of humility and gratitude:

> [The bonus] allows me to now…take care of the people that have given me this position and allowed this to happen. Like I always say, it is a team effort. A lot of behind the scenes work goes in when we're at home, when we're in the early stages and on course here. It's fantastic. I have an opportunity now, with a year like this and a bonus like that, to celebrate and to share it with the people that have made it possible… Our team did an unbelievable job this year. Everything was exactly how we needed it to be to peak at the right times. If we can continue to do that, then we'll have more seasons like this. (Kerr-Dineen 2015)

What is most remarkable about the comments of this humble "individual" athlete is how often he uses the word "we," and that he never once takes sole credit for the success. And so it is here that I wish to again acknowledge my team, particularly the brilliant Coach G, without whom this book would not exist.

Whether you are a team athlete or an individual athlete, list all the members of your team; include coaches, trainers, managers, equipment managers, family members, friends, officials, field-maintenance crews, janitors, and so on.

_____

_____

_____

_____

_____

Practice: Being of Service and Paying It Forward

When we are humble and acknowledge that our success depends on the support of others at least as much as it does on our own hard work, then we are often inspired to be of service and to pay it forward. The value of this habit of excellence is captured in the beautiful piece "The One Quality Great Teammates Have in Common," by John O'Sullivan, director of the Changing the Game Project:

"Coach, can I talk to you?"

"Sure," I said. "What's on your mind today, Michael?"

"Well, I just want to know what I can do so I get to start more games and get more playing time as a center midfielder. I don't think I am showing my best as a winger, and my parents tell me I am not going to get noticed by the college scouts unless something changes."

"Well, Michael," I said, "there is something that all coaches are looking for from the players they recruit. In fact, it is exactly what I am looking for from you as well. If you approach every practice, every fitness session, and every match with this one thing, I think you will see a huge improvement in your play, regardless of where you play. Interested?"

"Of course, coach. What is it?"

I waited a moment before I answered to make sure he was listening.

"You have to stop asking what you can get, and start asking what you can give. You must serve." (2015)

There are athletes who repeatedly choose to move beyond their small self to support their teammates and serve their team, their sport, and their community. These are athletes who recognize that it is a true privilege to pursue their passion, who aren't always looking for the next photo op, and who often serve in quiet ways out of the limelight.

For example, in 2012 Stephen Curry agreed to donate three malaria nets for every three-pointer he made. In doing so, he didn't just open his wallet, he opened his heart. Curry traveled to Tanzania and endured long, bumpy, dusty road trips and cheap hotels to hang nets, visit health clinics, and meet with both grieving mothers and royalty (D. Brown 2016). Curry's choice to be of service far away from the comforts of home, family, and the spotlight shows the heart of a true champion. He used his celebrity to give back, to improve the lives of others, to be of service.

Throughout history many famous athletes, and, perhaps more importantly, many athletes you haven't heard of, have served humanity, bravely taking a stand for acceptance, kindness, and justice in the face of hardship, discrimination, violence, and injustice. Here are just a few:

- Jesse Owens, winner of four gold medals in the 1936 Hitler-orchestrated Olympic games

- Carl "Luz" Long, German Olympic long jumper who encouraged Jesse Owens

- Gino Bartali, Italian cycling champ who risked his life cycling repeatedly across Italy during World War II to deliver false identification documents, saving eight hundred Jews

- Jackie Robinson, the first African American to play in the major leagues

- Kathrine Switzer, the first woman to register for and complete the Boston Marathon

- Tommie Smith and John Carlos, who raised their fists in the Black Power salute after winning gold and bronze, respectively, in the 200-meter sprint in the 1968 Olympics

- Peter Norman, a white Australian who wore an Olympic Project for Human Rights armband in solidarity with Smith and Carlos after winning the silver medal alongside them in 1968

- Muhammad Ali, an advocate for racial pride who was stripped of his boxing titles and prevented from competing for four years at the peak of his athletic career because he refused to participate in the Vietnam War

- Billie Jean King and Venus Williams, who advocated for and obtained equal pay for women tennis players at Wimbledon

- Nawal El Moutawakel, the first female Muslim athlete to win an Olympic gold medal, in the 400-meter hurdles in 1984

- Jason Collins and Michael Sam, the first openly gay NBA and NFL players, respectively

- Schuyler Bailar, the first openly transgender NCAA Division I athlete

- Missy Erickson, the national track-cycling champion who is bringing attention to the sexual abuse of young athletes

- Becky Hammon, the first female full-time assistant NBA coach

- Gregg Popovich, the first NBA head coach to hire a woman

- Members of the US women's soccer and hockey teams (and equally, if not more importantly, potential members of the US women's hockey team—had they agreed to cross the picket line) who stood together and advocated for equal pay for equal play

- Yuliya Stepanova (Russian Olympic 800-meter runner) and Tyler Hamilton (US Tour de France cyclist), elite athletes who doped and then chose to speak about the perils of performance-enhancing drugs

- Toby Atkins and Scott Mercier, cyclists you probably haven't heard of because they chose not to dope

- The hundreds of other athletes you probably haven't heard of because they chose not to dope

- Colin Kaepernick, the football player who chose to sit during the national anthem to bring attention to the long-standing injustice, discrimination, and abuse suffered by Black African Americans in the United States

I challenge you to make a commitment to serve. List one *new* way that you will serve in each of the following domains. It can be something simple, such as reaching out to a shy teammate, doing drills with a teammate returning after an injury, sitting with the person who sits alone at lunch, arranging to donate used athletic gear to the local Boys and Girls Club or a village in Africa.

Your team: _____

_____

Your school or workplace: _____

_____

Your community: _____

_____

Giving Yourself the Gift of Mindfulness

Occasionally, as in the examples in this chapter, habits of excellence, such as finishing and joy, conflict with each other. However, more often they reinforce each other. Below is a collection of the habits of excellence we have covered, and perhaps you can think of others; if you do, please email me at dramy@stillquietplace.com. Take a look at the habits, and commit to practicing one this week, or this month.

Filling emotional tanks   Humor

WHO KNOWS?

It's happening for me   Faith

PATIENCE   PERSEVERANCE

GRATITUDE   Responsibility

Preparedness   SERVICE

    SELF-COMPASSION

Flexibility   Integrity

Sportsmanship   Generosity   Joy

Compassion   HUMILITY

IMPERMANENCE   Equanimity

Forgiveness   Love of the game

Vigilance

CHAPTER 13

For the Love of the Game

Somewhere behind the athlete you've become, and the hours of practice, and the coaches who have pushed you is a little girl who fell in love with the game and never looked back... Play for her.

—Mia Hamm, Olympic and World Cup soccer champion

This chapter is the final chapter specifically for athletes. So, take some time for a closing guided reflection... Settle into stillness and quietness... Let the practices and ideas from this book that have been most useful to you, which have opened your mind and heart, bubble up into your awareness. Breathe, and reflect on what you have discovered about the following.

Resting in stillness and quietness: _____

_____

_____

Pause, and breathe...

Caring for your body: _____

_____

_____

Pause, and breathe...

Watching your thoughts: _____

_____

_____

Pause, and breathe…

Befriending your feelings:_____

_____

_____

Pause, and breathe…

Responding rather than reacting:_____

_____

_____

Pause, and breathe…

Facing challenges:_____

_____

_____

Pause, and breathe…

Mistakes and self-compassion:_____

_____

_____

Pause, and breathe…

Being a true teammate:_____

_____

_____

Pause, and breathe…

Almost moments:_____

_____

_____

Pause, and breathe…

Habits of excellence:_____

_____

_____

Pause, and breathe…

Loving the game:_____

_____

_____

If you'd like, you may email me your reflections and questions at dramy@stillquietplace.com, using "Athlete Reflection" as the subject line. I'd love to hear from you.

Basic Concept: Practice Makes…

Everyone has heard the cliché "Practice makes perfect." However, the truth is that with both athletic skill and the skills shared in this book, practice makes practice. And the more we practice, the more competent, confident, and fluid we become. Remember, there is *always* a next level, a refinement, a deeper experience of flow.

When you are ready to begin another developmental cycle of learning and moving toward flow, choose the practices you wish to focus on for the next week, month, or season. Remember, as with physical skills, you can't master everything at once. So, with kindness, curiosity, and honesty, choose your next sane and joyful step for developing your mental, emotional, and spiritual game. Choose one or two skills that you know you want to improve, or map out a progressive plan for the season.

Practice: Flashlight

The following practice combines many of the basic practices offered in the fundamental chapters into one simple form. You can download an audio recording of this practice at http://www.newharbinger.com/40217.

Find a relatively quiet, private place and make yourself comfortable.

When you're ready, settle in and close your eyes. Then turn on the flashlight of your attention and shine it on the breath and the Still Quiet Place between the breaths....

After a minute or so, gently shine the flashlight of your attention on sound, listening to sounds in the room, sounds beyond the room, and even sounds in your body—your breath, your heartbeat....

In your own time, shine the flashlight of attention on the body, noting where your body makes contact with the chair, the bed, your clothing, the air.... Noting areas that feel comfortable, uncomfortable, or neutral....feeling the general state, energy level, and specific sensations in the body....

Again, whenever you're ready, shine the flashlight of attention on thoughts, noticing thoughts as they come and go, with kindness and curiosity, bringing awareness to the quality and tone of thinking....

In your own time, shine the flashlight of attention on emotions, simply acknowledging whatever you're feeling in the moment....

Now, shine the flashlight of attention on the breath....

And then on the Still Quiet Place itself....

Just breathing and resting in stillness and quietness....

It can be very helpful to know that we have a flashlight of attention, that we can turn it on and choose where to focus it. We can expand the beam of our attention to include everything: the sights and sounds of the competitive venue and the roaring crowd, or we can narrow it to just the crucial elements of the moment: the ball, the defender and the goal, the test question, the person in front of us.... This ability to expand and narrow the flashlight of our attention is very helpful in many situations: during tryouts and competition, while taking a test or making a presentation, during a heated conversation, and the list goes on.

Activity: Love of the Game

Sometimes, as athletes and coaches, we become so focused on our performance that we lose sight of our original, natural, pure inspiration for participating. We lose our love of the game. While much of an athlete's life is hard work, blood, sweat, and tears, it is important to nurture and cultivate your love of the game. You can find this love by being fully in the present moment. It is experienced in the satisfying exhaustion after a grueling solitary workout, or when "nailing it" in the empty gym far away from the adoring crowds.

The simple words of an anonymous softball player demonstrate how mindfulness relates to her love of the game:

> You know you love the game when you walk on the field and…
> Forget about the drama going on at school.
> Forget the fight you had with your boyfriend earlier.
> Forget the scouts watching in the stands.
> Let everything go, and just focus on the game.
> That's a true athlete.

As George Mumford, author of *The Mindful Athlete*, writes, "The real question is this. How can you bring into your life, both on and off the court, the love of the game, the love of being present, the love of being all that you can be, the love of being of service, the love of taking your humanity to another level?" (2015, 203). Take some time to sit with this question, and discover your true answer. Possible answers include choosing to *be* in the present, surf the emotional waves, laugh off mistakes, step up your effort, practice PEACE, play with freedom, mentor a less experienced player, train or compete in another country, cross-train, step away from the game for a while, coach young kids at the recreation center, volunteer at the local hospital or animal shelter…

_____

_____

_____

Reflection: Beyond Competition

As athletes, we often think we are *competing against* our teammate for the starting spot, the clock, or our opponent for the win. Ultimately, we are competing, as Jim Wooden says, to "reveal our character" and to discover our best and most authentic self. And we do that by responding in the almost moments.

Unfortunately, as competitive athletes we often focus primarily on ourselves, our rankings, and our win-loss records. We are often consumed by our thinking, our feelings, our stories about ourselves as athletes, and our identity in our sport. We rarely step outside our small ego-based selves to experience flow.

I hope by now *you* have *realized* that you are much more than the position you play, your stats, your surgical scars, your trophies and memories. You are more than your thoughts and feelings and stories about yourself as an athlete. My friend Kristen Smyth, coach of the Stanford women's gymnastics team, reminds her athletes that they are much more than their sport:

> We try to teach [our gymnasts] that gymnastics is not who you are... It's a piece of what you do. It's all the qualities that you've developed through being a gymnast that [are] going to set you up for the rest of your life. And they go out into the world and find that next thing that they're going to fall in love with. (Kiefer, no date)

Not only does mindfulness increase our ability to achieve peak performance and find flow, but it also supports us in developing valuable qualities for the rest of our lives. However, ultimately, the true gift of becoming a mindful athlete is that you may discover your true essence. This experience is articulated by Shawn Green. As described previously, Green deliberately practiced skills like those offered in this book. In the process he became a multi-record-setting MLB player *and* a mindful athlete. He writes, "I always suspected there was more to my true essence than my incessant and repetitive thoughts and the insatiable desires of my ego...but it wasn't until that meditative work took root in my swing that I truly began to disconnect from my thoughts and connect with my deeper sense of being" (2011, 32).

Giving Yourself the Gift of Mindfulness

My sincerest wish is that in the process of reading this book you have come to realize that sports, particularly when done mindfully, are a way for you to move into the flow of the game, engage in the flow of life, and discover your true essence. Ultimately, you are pure stillness and quietness, joy and love!

To support your efforts to experience this, recommit to:

- Listening to the recorded practices

- Responding in almost moments

- Demonstrating habits of excellence

- Nurturing your love of the game

- Resting in stillness and quietness

PART 3

Skills for Coaches and Parents

The next two chapters are written for coaches and parents. They will support you in learning and applying many of the profoundly valuable skills your athlete/child practiced in the first two sections of this book. Specifically, these chapters will allow you to remember your highest intentions as a coach or a parent, to understand your coaching or parenting style from your athlete/child's perspective, and then to choose how you will coach or parent moving forward. Ultimately, this will improve your relationship with your athlete/ child, and increase the likelihood that she or he will find flow in sports and in life.

CHAPTER 14

For Coaches

A common mistake among those who work in sport is spending a disproportional amount of time on "x's and o's" as compared to time spent learning about people.

—Mike Krzyzewski, Duke University men's basketball coach and Olympic gold medal coach in 2008 and 2012

Thank you for reading this chapter. While I sincerely hope that you have read this book all the way through from the beginning, I realize that you may not have. So let's begin with a definition:

Mindfulness is paying attention here and now,
with kindness and curiosity,
so that we can choose our behavior.

Let's break this definition down. "Paying attention here and now" means not dwelling on the past or worrying about the future but paying attention to what's actually happening in *this* moment. And we pay attention "with kindness and curiosity"; otherwise, we can be incredibly hard on ourselves and our athletes. We tend to only see when we, and our athletes, have "made mistakes" or "screwed up." With mindfulness, we intentionally practice bringing an attitude of kindness and curiosity to ourselves and our experience. Finally, when we bring our kind and curious attention to our thoughts and feelings, to the sensations in our bodies, and to the people and circumstances in our lives, then we have everything we need "so that we can choose our behavior" and *respond* to challenging situations in training, competition, and daily life. Research on mindfulness and self-compassion in sports, academics, and the workplace indicates that these practices enhance the ability to learn, perform, and move toward mastery.

The same concepts, practices, reflections, and activities offered to athletes throughout this book can help *you* respond to typical coaching challenges. Specifically, they will support you as you provide your athletes with essential mental and emotional skills for training and competition; encourage athletes dealing with injuries and psychological challenges; work with insecure and arrogant athletes; enhance team chemistry; respond to player mistakes, bad calls by officials, and tough losses; deal with shortsighted, exceedingly optimistic (deluded), and overbearing parents; and address issues with staff. These skills will allow you to create a culture that will help individual athletes and the entire team to find flow and consistently perform their best.

Pause here and simply notice your thoughts and feelings as you reread the last statement: These skills will allow you to create a culture that will help individual athletes and the entire team to find flow and consistently perform their best.

As you begin, it may inspire you to know that many elite athletes and professional teams are enthusiastically using mindfulness, specifically because they have discovered that it enhances performance and creates the conditions for finding flow. See the "Mindfulness" section in chapter 1 for an incomplete list of the ever-growing number of athletes and teams who have used, or are using, mindfulness to enhance their performance.

If you are truly committed to sharing these skills with your athletes and you haven't read the rest of the book, I strongly encourage you to pause here and read chapter 1, "Welcome," and, at the very least, scan the table of contents to get a feel for the powerful mental and emotional skills offered in this book. While there is no way to capture all of the specifics and refinements offered in individual chapters, I will do my best to provide you with a working foundation.

Reflection: My Coaching

As a coach committed to excellence, you spend hours thinking about and planning the *what* of your coaching—the specific skills, drills, and progressions that you offer each day and throughout the season. Mindfulness invites you to explore the *why* and *how* of your coaching. So perhaps you can pause here, breathe, and reflect on your coaching, intentions, and methods. Be brave, be willing to be *real* with yourself, be kind and curious, and then see what you discover. Sit with each of the following questions for a few minutes, letting the layers of thoughts and feelings reveal themselves.

Why do you coach?

_____

_____

How were you coached?

_____

_____

How do you feel about how you were coached?

_____

_____

What qualities did you most appreciate in your coaches?

_____

_____

How do you define success?

_____

_____

What are your intentions when you coach?

_____

_____

How do you demonstrate these intentions on a daily basis?

_____

_____

What do you want your athletes to learn from you as a coach?

_____

_____

How would your athletes describe your coaching style?

_____

_____

Do you have coaching habits that you would like to change?

_____

_____

If you are feeling reluctant to really explore these topics, perhaps this story will encourage you to dig deeper. Dave Shaw, coach of the Stanford football team, was known for his stoicism. In fact, it inspired a campus T-shirt entitled "50 Shades of Shaw," on which "expressionless" faces of Shaw appeared above various emotions, such as excited, sad, confused, happy, and upset. During a 2014 game against UCLA, cornerback Ronnie Harris politely suggested that Shaw "loosen up." Harris told Shaw to "let it out. When you have a sense of comfort, place that in our hearts, as well." Harris's heartfelt comments prompted Shaw to modify his coaching style, that day and moving forward. The changes Shaw implemented inspired his players. Blake Martinez, an inside linebacker, noted the powerful impact of Shaw's more expressive style. "The thing I see is he gives us high-fives. We feed off that. It's like bonus motivation" (Wilner 2015).

Activity: Intentionally Creating the Culture

Each season you have the opportunity to establish team culture. What are your intentions? For yourself? For your athletes? For the team as a whole? As noted previously, *intentions* are distinct from goals, and they define qualities of being rather than specific outcomes. When intentions are held in the context of mindfulness, they serve as a behavioral compass. Here are a couple of examples of intentions: We treat ourselves, our teammates, our coaches, our opponents, and the officials with kindness and respect. We commit to coming to practice and games physically, mentally, and emotionally ready to play.

On the first day of the season it can be a fun and valuable team-building exercise to create a list of fifteen to twenty intentions, and then choose three to five intentions from the initial list to commit to for the season. Almost any topic in this book can be made into a guiding intention. You can refine this process by reflecting on qualities, or elements, that are missing or underdeveloped on your team. Many highly respected coaches will tell you in no uncertain terms that while their less successful colleagues are often technically very skilled, they are less successful *because they fail to develop an explicit, intentional team culture.*

Steve Kerr, coach of the Golden State Warriors, is a shining example of a coach who creates an intentional team culture. As mentioned already, the team's core values are joy, mindfulness, compassion, and competition—all topics covered in depth in earlier chapters (see Luke Walton's comments in the "Compassion" section, chapter 10).

Practice: The Magic Ratio and Filling Emotional Tanks

As the story about Stanford football coach Shaw demonstrates, *you* set the tone for your athletes and your team. A few words, or simple gestures, can inspire, or devastate, an athlete or an entire team. Research by Dr. John Gottman and others (Gottman 1994; Losada 1999; Losada and Heaphy 2004), highlighted previously (see "Positive Scanning and the Magic Ratio" and "Filling Your Teammates' Emotional Tanks"), shows that one-to-one relationships and teams function best if the ratio of positive to negative interactions is at least five to one. Sir Alex Ferguson, coach of Manchester United, unequivocally states, "Few people get better with criticism; most respond to encouragement instead. So I tried to give encouragement when I could. For a player—for any human being—there is nothing better than hearing 'Well done.' Those are the two best words ever invented" (Carmichael 2015).

So, are you willing to commit to maintaining the magic five-to-one ratio and to filling the emotional tanks of your athletes and staff (see chapters 5 and 10)? Are you hesitant? Are you concerned that doing so will make your team soft? If so, consider the following appreciative reflections about Steve Kerr, coach of the Golden State Warriors, from sports writer Noah Frank and Jim Thompson, founder of the Positive Coaching Alliance. Frank writes, "That's why the process of unyielding optimism, of always building up his players for the next challenge, rather than tearing them down for any failure, remains the most important aspect of his job." Thompson elaborates, "When you've got someone like Kerr right now, showing almost relentless positivity, it's fabulous… We want [coaches] to understand that positive emotions can create an upward spiral. What builds resilience is positivity" (Frank 2016).

Even if you are having doubts, simply commit to positive scanning and filling the emotional tanks of your athletes and staff for the next few weeks, and see what happens.

- When you are positive, what is the tone of the team on the field during training, water breaks, competition?

- Do their efforts and body language change?

- Are they more willing to push, take risks, and learn from mistakes?

Let's be clear. I am not suggesting that you offer overly cheerful false praise, or that there won't be moments when what is truly needed is clear, rigorous feedback—tough love. Rather, I am saying that when your athletes and staff trust you, and their tanks are full, then when you need to offer constructive criticism they won't be in fight, flight, or freeze mode (also known as the refractory period; see chapter 6); they will be able to *hear* your suggestions and will be *motivated* to act on them.

Activity: Attending to Individual Athletes

Most coaches work with several athletes; many coaches work with an entire team of athletes. Each athlete has her own personality and physical, mental, and emotional strengths and weaknesses. Early in the season, and at least once during the season, set aside time to reflect on each of your athletes. Do your best to see each athlete with fresh eyes. Initially, it can be helpful to acknowledge the basic story you tell yourself about your point guard, and then to consider other qualities she possesses. What are her strengths and weaknesses physically, mentally, and emotionally? What style of coaching is she most responsive to? How does she feel about her performance and her role on the team? How does she get along with her teammates? Is she a leader, a follower, a loner, a disruptive force? What do you know about her life outside of basketball? How is she doing in school? How are her relationships with her family, friends, roommates, and colleagues? How does she feel about her body? What qualities do you want to nurture in her? How can you best support her development as an athlete and a human being? Now that you have held her in your kind and curious attention, how might you coach her differently? Below are some specific examples of gifted coaches who mindfully attend to their athletes and modify their coaching accordingly.

Sir Alex Ferguson, coach of Manchester United, talks about mindfully observing and looking outside his usual boxes for each athlete (see "Thinking Outside the Box" in chapter 5) to pick up crucial information:

> Seeing a change in a player's habits, or a sudden dip in his enthusiasm allowed me to go further with him: Is it family problems? Is he struggling financially? Is he tired? What kind of mood is he in? Sometimes I could even tell that a player was injured when he thought he was fine. I don't think many people fully understand the value of observing. I came to see observation as a critical part of my management skills. The ability to see things is key—or, more specifically, the ability to see things you don't expect to see. (Carmichael 2015)

Coaches must be especially mindful of what individual athletes need, as well as how they respond to various coaching styles. Bill Walsh, former head coach of the San Francisco 49ers, offers an excellent example of mindfully coaching two unique quarterbacks. "Early on, we had to encourage Joe (Montana) to trust his spontaneous instincts. We were careful not to criticize him when he used his creative abilities and things did not work out. Instead, we nurtured him to use his instincts. We had to allow him to be wrong on occasion and to live with it. In the case of Steve (Young), it was almost the opposite. We had to work with him to be disciplined enough to live within the strict framework of what we were doing. Steve is a great spontaneous athlete and a terrific runner, but we found that we had to reduce the number of times he would use his instincts and increase his willingness to stay within the confines of the team concept."

Now you can practice the skill of attending to individual athletes by completing the following worksheet for each of your athletes. (You can download additional copies of the worksheet at http://www.newharbinger.com/40217.) Notice if you are tempted to blow off this drill. What would you say to an athlete who wanted to skip a particular drill?

ATTENDING TO INDIVIDUAL ATHLETES

What is the basic story you tell yourself about _____ (athlete's name)?

_____

_____

_____

What are this athlete's strengths and weaknesses physically, mentally, and emotionally?

_____

_____

_____

What style of coaching is this athlete most responsive to?

_____

_____

_____

How does this athlete feel about her or his performance and role on the team?

_____

_____

_____

How well does this athlete get along with teammates?

_____

_____

_____

Is this athlete a leader, a follower, a loner, or a disruptive force?

_____

_____

_____

How is this athlete doing in school or at work?

_____

_____

_____

How are this athlete's relationships with family, friends, roommates, or colleagues?

_____

_____

_____

How does this athlete feel about his or her body?

_____

_____

_____

What qualities do you want to nurture in this athlete?

_____

_____

_____

How can you best support this person's development as an athlete and a human being?

_____

_____

_____

Now that you have held this athlete in your kind and curious attention, how might you coach this person differently?

_____

_____

_____

Reflection: Attending to the Team as a Whole

If you are coaching a team, after you have reflected upon each athlete individually, expand your attention to consider the team as a whole.

How is team morale? How is the team's energy level? If it is low, would the team benefit from a period of recovery, a more playful practice, or an increase in intensity? If it is high, is it sustainable through the season or does it need to be tempered slightly?

Watch your athletes as they arrive and depart from practice, partner for drills, recover during water breaks, hang out on the bus, and unwind at meals. What is the general tone of the team? Is the banter lighthearted and inclusive? Is there an undercurrent of tension, resentment, or cliquishness? Do players mix and match, or are there repetitive divisions?

This type of reflection is absolutely critical to getting the most out of your team. In highly competitive environments, if a culture of inclusivity and cooperation is not *actively cultivated* on a moment-to-moment basis, players often engage in an insidious and invisible form of bullying known as relational aggression or emotional bullying. Ideally, the environment on a team is one of true cooperation and compassion (operating together, sharing a passion), which brings out the best in each person. As noted on the Proactive Coaching Facebook page, "Good teams don't have an 'in group' and an 'out group.' Leadership must prevent this by developing an intentional culture and then keeping their arms around the whole team and insisting the players do as well. Everyone matters on great teams" (2015).

It is beyond heartbreaking to hear athletes as young as eight describe textbook cases of ongoing, unaddressed relational aggression on local soccer teams, and to read about the pervasive, extremely cruel culture of bullying on some NFL teams (Van Bibber 2014). Slowly, athletes, parents, and coaches are becoming aware of and addressing this epidemic that manifests itself in thousands of *almost* invisible interactions every day on fields and courts and in pools and locker rooms across the country.

Relational aggression, also known as emotional bullying, is using relationships to cause emotional pain. It is a subtle and extremely difficult-to-detect pattern of behavior directed at one or two individuals. The most common manifestations are excluding from social groups and activities, mean teasing, rumor spreading, secret divulging, alliance building, backstabbing, ignoring, verbal insulting, and using hostile body language (for example, eye rolling and smirking). Simple examples of relational aggression that may occur on teams include teammates rejecting a request to partner with or sit with a particular individual, and then happily partnering or sitting with a preferred, more popular teammate, or a teammate sharing snacks with everyone except one or two individuals. Another telltale sign of relational aggression is an athlete trying to defend or justify cruel behavior by saying, "I was just kidding. Can't you take a joke?"

Athletes engage in relational aggression to feel better about themselves and to elevate their social status, while simultaneously diminishing the social status of the victim and isolating this person. Relational bullies are driven by jealousy, competitiveness, insecurity, and desire for approval. They engage in this type of bullying specifically because it is extremely difficult to detect and is thus likely to remain both unnoticed and unaddressed. Athletes who *appear* the most innocent may be the most cruel. These bullies are often popular, charismatic "leaders" who are well liked by adults (Yoon, Barton, and Taiariol 2004).

Emotional bullying has a significant negative impact on each athlete and the team as a whole. Obviously the victims suffer. What is less obvious, however, is that the bystanders and bullies also suffer. Bystanders live in fear that they will be the next to be bullied, and they feel conflicted because they are unsure how to intervene. Bullies suffer because they know in their hearts that their behavior is unkind and destructive.

It is important to understand that the impulse beneath bullying is most often deep-seated insecurity. As a coach, it is *your* responsibility to coach constructively (so that your athletes feel good about themselves and don't need to build themselves up by bullying others), to create an inclusive team culture, and to set clear expectations about how you want your athletes to treat each other on and off the court or playing field. There are two reasons why it is crucial that you coach in this manner. First, it is the right thing to do. Second, individual athletes and the entire team will perform better if every athlete feels safe, respected, included, and cared for by you and his or her teammates. The necessity of this type of atmosphere is summed up by Phil Jackson, champion NBA basketball player and coach, who writes, "It takes a number of critical factors to win an NBA championship, including the right mix of talent, creativity, intelligence, toughness, and of course, luck. But if a team doesn't have the most essential ingredient—love—none of those other factors matter" (2014, 4).

When you look through the lens of relational aggression, or emotional bullying, do you have any concerns about your team? Have you seen *any* red-flag behaviors?

If you have seen *anything*, even "little" signs, something that you might be tempted to write off as an isolated incident or as no big deal, continue observing. Bullies are sneaky, and unless you are paying extremely close attention, their actions will be undetectable and invisible. What you see is always the snowflake on the tip of the iceberg.

One way to assess whether relational bullying is an issue on your team is to have your players *anonymously* complete the "if you spot it, you got it" practice in chapter 10. Additionally, basic athlete, coach, and parent agreements are provided with the online resources (visit http://www.newharbinger.com/40217). I drafted these agreements while creating team-building and antibullying workshops for the Positive Coaching Alliance. You can adapt the agreements to your own coaching style and circumstances.

Practice: Three Questions to Build Connection

Even if you think your team's relationships are in great shape, on a lighter practice day it can be extremely beneficial to have your athletes play the game of three questions. To begin, have them make two lines facing each other and pair off. Invite them to close their eyes and rest in stillness and quietness. Then, offer the following instructions:

Okay, for this drill, the players with their back to the goal are going to be the speakers, and the players facing the goal are going to be the listeners. I am going to read three questions. After each question the speaker is going to respond. And the listener is going to…? Yep, just listen. Listen from the heart, and notice any thoughts or feelings that arise while the speaker is responding. After the speaker has answered all three questions, we will switch, and repeat the process with the listener becoming the speaker. The intention of this practice is to support you in becoming a more cohesive, effective team. The more real you are willing to be with each other, the more likely that is to happen. So be brave, and be honest.

Allow at least one to two minutes for the speaker to respond to each of the following questions:

What do we have in common?

What do you appreciate about me?

What do you want me to know?

Depending on how brave and real you want your players to be, you can encourage them to be a bit more vulnerable, modifying the last question to suit your circumstances:

What do you want me to know about you?

What do you want me to know about how we can best work together?

What do you want me to know about myself as a teammate?

After the first person has responded, repeat the process for the second person. Once each person in the first pairing has responded to the questions, have all the players pause, close their eyes, breathe, reset, then shuffle one player to the right. Repeat the process until each player has answered the three questions with each teammate. To close, again have them pause, breathe, and open their hearts, a bit more, to each player on the team. It is only when athletes know and trust each other that they are able to perform at their best, especially in decisive situations. Theo Epstein, president of the Chicago Cubs, believes trust, vulnerability, and connection allowed his team to win the 2016 World Series:

> We were winners that night in Cleveland because when things went really, really wrong—and then the rains came—our players already knew each other so well that they could come together; they already trusted each other so much that they could open up and be vulnerable, and they were already so connected that they could lift one another up. We had already won. (*Time* Staff 2017)

Practice: Responding Rather Than Reacting

The early chapters of this book are devoted to supporting athletes in building the skills to respond (pause and choose their behavior) rather than react (act immediately out of upset and habit) in challenging situations. As a coach, you can use these same skills to respond to the unique difficulties that arise during the season—responding to players' mistakes, officials' bad calls, tough losses, and conflicts within the team, with parents, and with your staff. Charles R. Swindoll, pastor, author, and educator, writes that "life is 10 percent of what happens to me and 90 percent of how I react (or respond) to it." Again, I strongly encourage you to read the early sections of this book, so that you can learn the fundamentals of responding and *then* share them with your athletes.

Here's an example of two coaches behaving differently when their kickers missed field goals in the same NFL game. On October 23, 2016, the Arizona Cardinals and Seattle Seahawks game ended in a 6–6 tie. During the game, kickers Chandler Catanzaro (Cardinals) and Stephen Hauschka (Seahawks) each missed makeable field goals. During the postgame press conference, when asked about the missed field goal, Cardinals head coach Bruce Arians responded, "Make it. This is professional, this ain't high school, baby. You get paid to make it."

Seahawks coach Pete Carroll had a different take on his kicker's miss, saying that Hauschka "made his kicks to give us a chance and unfortunately he didn't make the last one. He's been making kicks for years around here…but he's gonna hit a lot of winners as we go down the road here. I love him and he's our guy" (Bariso 2016).

Which coach reacted?

Which coach responded?

Which coach publicly promotes mindfulness?

Which kicker is most likely to be in flow and perform optimally the next time out?

Remember that how *you* respond teaches your athletes how to respond to mistakes, injuries, and other difficulties. Practice responding like Pete Carroll did, with acceptance, composure, and confidence, and your athletes will do the same.

Activity: Mindful Communication

As many of the wise coaches quoted in this chapter have indicated, ultimately coaching is about relationships, and relationships are built one communication at a time. Because relationships involve people and their thoughts, feelings, stories, fears, and desires, difficult communications are inevitable. Knowing this, you can minimize difficulties by practicing mindful communication and by encouraging your players, staff, and parents to do the same. (See "Mindful Communication" in chapter 10 for a detailed explanation of this practice.)

In short, mindful communication means that in challenging situations, when things get messy, you take some time to breathe and allow your thoughts (see chapter 5), feelings (see chapter 6), stories, fears, and desires to arise and fall away, and *then* you *choose* your words wisely.

Can you wait until the waves of frustration (see chapters 6 and 10)—yours and your athletes'—have subsided, and then ask yourself the following?

- Is your athlete (or team members) in a place where he (or they) can really hear you?

- What is your intention for the conversation?

- What do you want the athlete or team to learn?

- *How* do you want to convey your message?

- Are there *specific* physical or tactical qualities—speed, conditioning, dribbling, passing, shooting, positioning and movement, offensive skills (one-on-one or combination), defensive stance, reading the game—that the player or team needs to develop?

- What habits of excellence are missing?

The most difficult conversation is often the one when you have to tell a player that he is not performing—physically, mentally, emotionally, or in relation to teammates or coaching staff—at the level needed. Although these conversations can be tough, if they are done with intention, clarity, and compassion they can provide athletes with a crucial almost moment (see chapter 11), which requires them to choose whether and how they wish to move forward.

What follows is a description of a difficult conversation that Chris Petrucelli, the US Women's National Under-21 soccer coach, had with Carli Lloyd in 2003. He had to inform Lloyd that she was being cut from the team:

> I remember saying to her, "You're really talented, but there are holes in your game that need to be fixed if you're going to be a national team player… At this point, you're not ready, but here are some things you have to do."
>
> This is where Lloyd was supposed to react [or rather respond] and prove Petrucelli wrong. That would come later. Much later. (Carlisle 2015)

As you probably know, this wasn't the end of the story for Carli. Eventually she came to understand that this conversation was a pivotal almost moment (chapter 11) in her development as a player, and that the conversation happened for her, not to her (see "It Is Happening for Me, Not to Me," chapter 8). Reflecting on having been cut, she said, "It was the first time a coach gave me some tough love, and I needed it" (Carlisle 2015). In 2015, after more than a decade of extremely disciplined work she scored three beautiful goals in the World Cup final and was named FIFA Player of the Year.

Basic Concept: Player-to-Player Communication

Have you explicitly discussed with your players how you want them to communicate with each other? During competition? Outside the competitive arena? When things are going well? When they are having difficulties? Are you encouraging them to use the magic ratio (chapter 5) and to fill emotional tanks (chapter 10)? Have you experimented with running a practice in silence so they can read the game and communicate nonverbally? Have you run drills in which each player must say something positive before passing the ball or the puck?

Take a moment and consider the specifics of constructive team communication during competition.

Effective communication in the heat of the moment is PDQ:

- Positive: The player (or coach) giving instructions says what he wants his teammate to do ("Cut off the angle"), rather than what he doesn't want him to do ("Don't get beat").

- Direct: The instructions are clear and specific ("diagonal run"), rather than vague ("Go!").

- Quick: The instructions are quick and easy to understand.

More complex issues are best addressed off the field using the mindful communication practice in chapter 10.

Giving Your Team the Gift of Mindfulness

If you set clear intentions; establish an inclusive and cooperative environment; train your athletes' minds and hearts as well as their bodies; maintain the magic five-to-one ratio and fill your athletes' emotional tanks; support them in dealing with mistakes, challenges, setbacks, and injuries; respond rather than react; communicate mindfully; and cultivate habits of excellence and a love of the game, then your athletes will perform at their best, whether they are third-graders or Olympians.

CHAPTER 15

For Parents

I don't think parents can "make" professional athletes, but they certainly can destroy them by taking away a kid's joy.

—Matt Birk, Pro Bowl center for the Minnesota Vikings and Baltimore Ravens

Thank you for reading this chapter. I assume that you are reading it because you are truly committed to supporting your child in all aspects of life, including sports. While I hope that you have read this book all the way through from the beginning, I realize that you may not have. So, for your ease, I have included cross-references to relevant sections. To ensure we are on the same page, we will begin with a definition, followed by an introductory practice designed specifically for parents with children who play sports. Now for the definition:

Mindfulness is paying attention here and now,
   with kindness and curiosity,
   so that we can choose our behavior.

The dilemma for all of us who want to support our children in their various endeavors is that often our perceptions about our motivations and our behaviors are profoundly different from our children's *experience* of them. Put simply, what we intend as *support* is often experienced by our children as PRESSURE. Research shows that such pressure negatively affects our children—causing performance anxiety, decreased enjoyment of the sport, sport burnout, and eventually sport drop out. More importantly, this pressure can increase the risk of physical injury, anxiety, and depression and ultimately can have negative, lifelong effects on our relationships with our children and on their health and well-being.

First, simply take some slow deep breaths, and then bring your kind and curious attention to the physical sensations, thoughts, and feelings that arise as you reread these salient points from the preceding paragraph.

What we intend as *support* is often experienced by our children as PRESSURE. Research shows that such pressure negatively affects our children—causing performance anxiety, decreased enjoyment of the sport, sport burnout, and eventually sport drop out. More importantly, this pressure can increase the risk of physical injury, anxiety, and depression and ultimately can have negative, lifelong effects on our relationships with our children and on their health and well-being.

What sensations did you feel in your body?

_____

_____

What thoughts appeared in your mind?

_____

_____

What feelings arose in your heart?

_____

_____

Maybe your experience was along the lines of *I am not one of those parents, and this doesn't apply to me.* Or perhaps it was *Uh oh, this might be me.* Or maybe it was *I know I am pushing my kid, and it is for his own good.* Just breathe and notice your response with kindness and curiosity...

Now that the initial reaction has subsided, you have a choice. You can continue to interact with your child as you have in the past, or you can open your heart and begin a gentle inquiry; then, at the end of this chapter, you can choose *how* you will engage with your child moving forward.

If you are still reading, I assume that you have wisely chosen to explore this complex territory. So let's begin.

Activity: Your Data

Let's begin by collecting some data. It would be easy to skim this section, telling yourself you'll just do it in your head. If you are *truly* committed to supporting your child and helping her find flow, I encourage you to make time for sincere self-reflection. Please go slow; be kind, curious, and rigorously honest; and actually *write down your answers.* Having written answers will be essential when you speak with your child.

What are your goals and hopes for you child in his or her chosen sport?

_____

_____

What do you hope your child will learn through participating in sports?

_____

_____

How important is it to you that your child succeed in sport?

_____

_____

When your child plays well, wins, or makes the team, what do you do and say?

_____

_____

When your child plays poorly, loses, or gets cut, what do you do and say?

_____

_____

What do you say about other players, parents, coaches, referees, and opponents when your child or child's team wins?

_____

_____

What do you say about other players, parents, coaches, referees, and opponents when your child or child's team loses?

_____

_____

What stories do you tell about various situations regarding your child and sports, especially situations when things don't go the way you and your child had hoped?

_____

_____

_____

_____

For advanced practice, consider your facial expression and body language in each of the above situations.

What do your facial expression and body language convey?

_____

_____

Are your words, facial expressions, and body language giving a consistent message?

_____

_____

If not, know that the body doesn't lie, and actions, even small gestures, speak much louder than words.

And now, let's take this exploration one step further.

If your child could speak freely, how would she describe her experience regarding your involvement in her sport?

_____

_____

_____

Okay. Deep breath. How are you feeling right now? Can you simply breathe into the feelings and allow them to be just as they are in this moment?

Now you have some information and an initial response to that information. Perhaps you are feeling good about how you are supporting your child. Perhaps you are feeling skeptical about this reflective process, or defensive about your behaviors. This is a good place to pause and simply allow your experience to be as it is. There's nothing to prove, defend, or protect. Simply offer yourself openhearted exploration, kindness, and curiosity.

Activity: Your Child's Data

Now it is time to check in with your child. It is entirely possible that your child feels loved and supported by you. And it is also possible that the actions you intend to be loving and supportive are *experienced* by your child as pressure, perhaps even extreme pressure. Either way, once you know what is true for your child, then you can *choose* whether you want to continue or change your behaviors. Notice if you are reluctant to receive feedback from your child. Then, as Nike says, "Just do it," and do it with kindness and curiosity.

If your child is reluctant to offer feedback, this is cause for concern and an indication that you may want to have a skilled neutral party facilitate this discussion. The questions in this section will allow your child to share his or her experience with you, and, if you are open, help you understand that experience.

To begin this conversation, you can say something along the lines of:

I really want to support you in whatever you choose to pursue, be it sports, academics, music, art—whatever. And I realize that there is a difference between support and pressure. So I want to check in and really learn what is most supportive for you. It would help me if you would take some time to answer some questions about your experience of my involvement in your sport, and then share your answers with me.

What are your parent's goals and hopes for you in your chosen sport?

_____

_____

What does your parent hope you will gain and learn by participating in sports?

_____

_____

How important is it to your parent that you succeed in your sport?

_____

_____

When you play well, win, or make the team, what does your parent do and say?

_____

_____

When you play poorly, lose, or are cut from the team, what does your parent do and say?

_____

_____

What does your parent say about other players, parents, coaches, referees, and opponents when your team wins?

_____

_____

What does your parent say about other players, parents, coaches, referees, and opponents when your team loses?

_____

_____

What stories does your parent tell about various situations involving you and your sport, especially situations when things don't go the way you or your parent had hoped?

_____

_____

What do your parent's facial expression and body language convey in relation to your sport?

_____

_____

Do your parent's words, facial expressions, and body language match and give a consistent message?

_____

_____

If you had to summarize the message that your parent's comments and behaviors convey about your participation in sports, what would you say in one to two sentences?

_____

_____

_____

_____

What does your parent say or do that feels stressful to you?

_____

_____

_____

_____

What does your parent do, or what could your parent do, that would feel supportive to you?

_____

_____

_____

_____

Is there anything you would like your parent to change about how he or she is involved in your sport, such as not critique you after a competition, come to more games, stop shaking his head, tell you three positive things after each competition, stop yelling instructions? As you consider your answer, be as specific as possible.

_____

_____

_____

_____

Practice: Listening with Love for Understanding

Parent, now that you and your child have each had a chance to reflect on your involvement in his sport, you can sit down together to explore his experience. An extremely well-done study assessing junior tennis players' preferences for parental behaviors states that "parents would benefit from engaging their children in discussions to identify what behaviors they find are supportive when they are competing and what behaviors they find pressuring or unhelpful" (Knight, Boden, and Holt 2010). Remember, extensive research shows that:

- Compared to their children, parents overestimate their level of support and underestimate their level of pressure (Yesu and Harwood 2015).

- The more pressure a child experiences, the less he enjoys his sport (Kanters, Bocarro, and Casper 2008).

- The less a child enjoys her sport, the more likely she is to drop out (Kanters, Bocarro, and Casper 2008).

- Parents who believe they are creating a positive environment for their child to excel in and enjoy sports may in fact be contributing to their child's withdrawal from sports (Kanters, Bocarro, and Casper 2008).

So keeping in mind (and heart) that it is very likely that your child feels more pressured than you think, take a deep breath and *commit* to

- meeting your child exactly as she is in this moment;

- noticing any defensiveness on your part, and any impulse to explain, justify, or say "Yes, but…";

- letting the above *reactions* runs their course; and

- *choosing* to open your heart and really *hear* and *honor* your child.

Now invite your child to share her answers to the questions with you. Your job in this process is to *listen* with an open, undefended heart; to step into your child's experience; and to hear what she says.

Pause here. After you have listened to your child, continue reading.

Hopefully, you have now really heard your child. Maybe she feels truly supported by you. Maybe he feels more pressured than you realized. Either way, now you can use this valuable information to consider what drives your behavior so you can catch your pressuring behaviors in real time and, most importantly, practice making more supportive choices moment by moment.

Reflection: How Did We Get Here?

Remember when your child was young? Did you clap with delight as she took her first steps? Did you kiss her knee when she fell and scraped it? Did she learn to walk because you were giving her specific, detailed instructions about how to balance her weight and move her feet? Or did she learn naturally, on her own, through falling down and picking herself up over and over again? Looking back, can you see a transition from support to pressure, even if it was subtle?

In chapter 5, "Getting Your Head in the Game," your child learned to watch thoughts without believing them or taking them personally. What thoughts and stories lead us to pressure our children?

There are at least three very common thoughts that contribute to us pressuring our kids. So pause here, breathe, and, with kindness and curiosity, notice what sensations arise in your body, what thoughts arise in your mind, and what feelings arise in your heart as you read the next three sentences.

He has potential.

Breathe…

She could get a scholarship.

Breathe…

He could go pro.

Breathe…

Maybe your body feels at ease, and you think, *Yeah, that would be great. We'll see*, and you feel slightly excited. Or maybe there is more intensity, a restless, nervous energy in your body, and you think, *She really needs to train more. I'll set up some private sessions with the coach of the top team*, and you feel anxious. It's all good. There is nothing to judge, or change, or fix. And if your experience is more like the second example, your child is probably feeling more pressure than support.

Before we move on, take another look at the three sentences. Are they based in the past? The present? Or the future? Yup. They're all based in the future, and for all of us—athletes, parents, human beings—most of our stress, anxiety, and pressure come from being overly focused on the future.

Basic Concept: Scholarships—The Reality

So let's pause here and step out of the future fantasies and into present-moment realities regarding the holy grail of youth sports (at least in the United States)—the Division I college scholarship. When our children are young, it is relatively easy for us to simply be supportive and encouraging. As they grow up, especially if they begin to excel in a particular sport, it can become increasingly difficult for us to maintain perspective and not get overly attached to specific outcomes, particularly the elusive college scholarship.

Just how elusive is a college scholarship in your child's chosen sport? The information in the following tables comes directly from the NCAA. The tables show the number of high school athletes who compete in each sport by gender, and the percentage of high school athletes who go on to compete in each sport in each NCAA division. For an increasing number of sports, many of the most competitive athletes seeking scholarships choose to play on elite travel teams rather than their high school team. For such sports, the numbers in the tables underestimate the number of players competing for scholarships, and they therefore overestimate the percentage of players receiving scholarships. And, stating the obvious, only a *very select few* within each sport move on from college to compete at the professional or Olympic level (Bonesteel 2015; NCAA 2017).

Men's NCAA Scholarships

	High School Participants	NCAA Participants	Overall Percentage of High School Participants to NCAA	Percentage of High School Participants to Division I	Percentage of High School Participants to Division II	Percentage of High School Participants to Division III
Baseball	486,567	34,198	7.0	2.1	2.2	2.7
Basketball	541,479	18,697	3.5	1.0	1.0	1.4
Cross- Country	250,981	14,330	5.7	1.9	1.4	2.3
Football	1,083,617	72,788	6.7	2.6	1.8	2.4
Golf	148,823	8,654	5.8	2.0	1.7	2.1
Hockey	35,875	4,071	11.3	4.6	0.5	6.3
Lacrosse	108,450	13,165	12.1	2.9	2.2	7.1
Soccer	432,569	24,477	5.7	1.3	1.5	2.8
Swimming	137,087	9,715	7.1	2.8	1.1	3.2
Tennis	157,240	8,211	5.3	1.7	1.1	2.4
Track and Field	578,632	28,177	4.9	1.9	1.2	1.7
Volleyball	54,418	1,818	3.3	0.7	0.8	1.8
Water Polo	21,626	1,044	4.8	2.6	0.7	1.5
Wrestling	258,208	7,049	2.7	1.0	0.7	1.0

Women's NCAA Scholarships

	High School Participants	NCAA Participants	Overall Percentage of High School Participants to NCAA	Percentage of High School Participants to Division I	Percentage of High School Participants-to Division II	Percentage of High School Participants to Division III
Basketball	429,504	16,589	3.9	1.2	1.1	1.6
Cross-Country	221,616	16,150	7.3	2.7	1.7	2.8
Field Hockey	60,549	5,894	9.7	2.9	1.2	5.7
Golf	72,582	5,221	7.2	3.0	2.1	2.1
Ice Hockey	9,418	2,175	23.1	9.0	1.1	13.1
Lacrosse	84,785	10,994	13.0	3.7	2.5	6.7
Soccer	375,681	26,995	7.2	2.4	1.9	2.9
Softball	364,103	19,628	5.4	1.7	1.6	2.1
Swimming	166,838	12,428	7.4	3.2	1.1	3.1
Tennis	182,876	8,960	4.9	1.6	1.1	2.2
Track and Field	478,726	28,797	6.0	2.7	1.5	1.8
Volleyball	432,176	17,026	3.9	1.2	1.2	1.6
Water Polo	19,204	1,152	6.0	3.5	1.1	1.4

A study entitled "Sports and Health in America" (NPR, Robert Wood Johnson Foundation, and Harvard T. H. Chan School of Public Health 2015) found that 26 percent of parents of high school athletes hope their kids go on to play professional sports. This study was accurately summarized in the *Washington Post* as follows: "In other news, 26 percent of parents of high school athletes are delusional, because the odds that their kids go on to the professional ranks are absurdly low" (Bonesteel 2015).

Again, pause here and check in with yourself. Be brave and honest. What is happening in your body, mind, and heart? Even when we know the statistics, we often have a sense of agitation in the body, feel anxious or defensive, and think, *Yes, and my kid is one of the few who has a real shot*. And maybe your child does.

But here's the thing: if your child does have a shot, you need to know that savvy coaches evaluate players on far more than their stats. According to Lisa Heffernan and Jennifer Wallace (2016), the best coaches and teams are looking for players who can face challenges (chapter 8) with resilience and grace, who can demonstrate sportsmanship and integrity (chapter 11), who are committed to being steadfast teammates (chapter 10), who cultivate habits of excellence (chapter 12), and who truly love the game (chapter 13). Theo Epstein, president of the Chicago Cubs, the 2016 World Series winners, reiterates these points:

> Early in my career, I used to think of players as assets, statistics on a spreadsheet… The truth—as our team proved in Cleveland—is that a player's character matters. The heartbeat matters. Fears and aspirations matter. The player's impact on others matters. The tone he sets matters. The willingness to connect matters. Breaking down cliques and overcoming stereotypes in the clubhouse matters. Who you are, how you live among others—that all matters. (*Time* Staff 2017)

As you might have guessed, parental pressure usually kills qualities that coaches are seeking, whereas parental support nurtures them.

Now, what if your child really doesn't have a shot at a scholarship, finds another passion, or gets seriously injured? What do you want her to have learned from all her hours on the field, in the gym, at the rink, or in the pool? What skills are going to help her perform at her best and joyfully share her gifts in her career, friendships, family, and community? Fortunately, the skills listed previously that will help her get a scholarship are exactly the same skills that will allow her to thrive when she no longer competes. Simply put, supporting your child to cultivate mindfulness and develop habits of excellence will not only help her be recruited, but it will also help her if she is not recruited, and as she moves through life. So there is absolutely everything to gain.

Reflection: You're Being Evaluated Too

There is one more consideration. The number of sophisticated coaches and recruiters who consider parents and the athlete-parent interaction in their recruitment process is rapidly increasing. Coaches and scouts are assessing *your* behavior and *your* social media posts. Pat Fitzgerald, head football coach at Northwestern University, notes, "When we talk about our fit, we're evaluating the parents, too. And if the parents don't fit, then we might punt on the player and not end up offering him a scholarship" (Bastie 2017). So not only do you want your child to practice mindfulness, but you also want to practice it yourself. You want to practice checking your ego and attachment to your child's performance at the venue entrance; responding rather than reacting (chapter 7) when things don't go as hoped; and *thinking* (chapter 11) before you rag on a teammate, coach, or ref in public or via social media.

Reflection: Why Practice Mindfulness?

Just notice which of the preceding topics most motivated you to cultivate supportive attitudes and behaviors:

- Are you motivated to support your child's practice of mindfulness and development of habits of excellence because it will help him get a scholarship, or because it will help him later in life, or both?

- Are you motivated to practice mindfulness because it will help your child get a scholarship, because it will help you be more supportive of your child, because it will help you in your daily life, or all of the above?

Again, whatever is true for you is fine. Just be honest with yourself. You can only make wise choices about your behavior when you tell yourself the truth.

Reflection: Recognizing When We Pressure Our Children

As you may have guessed, the early parts of this chapter are based on the probability that you—like parents in the research studies and daily news stories, and like me, occasionally…or frequently—cross the line from being supportive to pressuring your child.

It's human. And if we are aware of our tendencies, we can pause and choose our behavior.

Please know I am not suggesting that you are like the extreme parents featured in various news stories, or that you don't want what is truly best for your child on all levels. It is just that sometimes our love of our children, our love of the game, and our fantasies about the future combine in such a way that we lose our perspective. I know I have lost perspective at times. So it is good to check in with yourself, and with your child, from time to time, to make sure you haven't lost your way.

Checking in with yourself involves bringing awareness to the body (chapter 3), watching thoughts (chapter 5), and befriending feelings (chapter 6). If you notice an agitated, anxious physical-emotional energy, with racing thoughts, you are likely overinvested, and this increases the odds that you will pressure your child. Our children will be more likely to find flow if we heed this sage warning from Brandi Chastain: "More often than not, to the child a gentle push feels like a shove" (2004, 45).

Here's my story. I have two children. My son began cycling competitively at the age of thirteen and has been entirely self-motivated and extremely dedicated to his training; at age eighteen he began racing professionally. Through most of junior high, my daughter played on highly competitive travel teams and truly *loved* soccer. At some point, her interests shifted to music and theater. Because my passion is sports, I didn't see, or create the space for her to communicate, her new passion. There was a period of time when I didn't fully acknowledge my attachment to her playing soccer. Yet, if I am honest, I could *feel* an undercurrent of pushing energy. It showed up in my body as an eager anticipation, in my mind as hopes and worries, and in my behavior in the loaded way I would ask supposedly neutral questions.

Fortunately, Coach G (see the introduction) stepped in. First, she supported my daughter in owning her truth; then she supported me in opening my heart and really hearing my daughter. Thankfully, my daughter is now learning life lessons and finding flow through music and theater. And sometimes I notice that pushing, desperate energy regarding my son's cycling, my daughter's college-application process, and my own professional opportunities, including writing this book. When I feel this particular energy, I do my best to observe it with kindness and curiosity, to allow it to pass, and then to choose my next sane and joyful step (chapter 8).

The preceding passage is not meant to suggest that we should or will feel neutral about our child's sports experience, or that support doesn't sometimes have a tough love quality. Rather, the invitation is for you to learn to recognize *your* attachment to and investment in a particular outcome, and to learn to accept the highs and lows of your child's sports experience with the same equanimity he learned in chapter 8. Ultimately, our job is to help our children to be in their bodies, to watch their thoughts, to befriend their feelings, to respond to difficulties, to face challenges, to learn from mistakes, to act with integrity, to be good teammates, to develop habits of excellence, and, most importantly, to nurture their love of the game regardless of a particular outcome. And it is only by *practicing* these skills ourselves that we can support our children in doing the same.

Practice: Choosing Your Behavior

If you want to step clearly into the domain of support, or if (based on your answers to the questions at the beginning of the chapter, your discussions with your child, and your physical sensations, thoughts, feelings, and behaviors) you suspect that you have repeatedly crossed the line from supporting to pressuring, then commit to working *mindfully* with the following supportive practices. As a gentle reminder, *working mindfully* means paying attention, here and now, with kindness and curiosity to our experience, so that we can choose our behavior. As you do the exercises, notice

- what happens in your body, mind, and heart and with your behavior;

- any resistance to the practices, including *Yes, but…* or *I'll just make this one comment* type of thinking;

- when you mindlessly revert to old habits;

- your child's response (more relaxed, at ease, lighthearted, willing to take risks);

- any shifts in your relationship with your child, his teammates, parents of teammates, opponents, and coaches;

- how it feels to simply *be* at a competition knowing that you are only going to express specific supportive sentiments in both your words and actions; and then,

- when old habits creep in, simply smile at yourself and recommit to the practices.

Just like when your child is learning a new physical, mental, or emotional skill, developing these new sports-parenting skills to the point where they are reliable in clutch situations will take committed, repeated practice. Are you willing to make the same commitment to developing these skills that your child is making to develop his?

Positives from the Past

The first season I coached for the American Youth Soccer Organization (AYSO), the head coach had a policy that during games we could only make positive statements about actions that had happened in the past. Sadly, he implemented this rule because he recognized that his extremely intense coaching had driven his very talented teenage daughter from the sport, and he did not want to make the same mistake with his six-year-old daughter. This type of parental coaching is not uncommon. Olympic and World Cup soccer champion Brandi Chastain remembers her own father's challenging style of coaching: "My dad was on the ref and was also yelling at me. I felt my soccer instincts were guiding me, but every time I heard his voice, I couldn't get anything done. He was trying to help but it just made me unable to function" (2004, 47).

I loved my AYSO coach's rule for positive coaching and took it as a challenge. You can get a surprising amount of simple "coaching" done following this rule. "Nice pass!" "I love how you're talking to each other!" "Great hustle!" "Beautiful defense!" While this rule is definitely not sufficient for higher-level coaching, it is ideal for supportive parenting. It prevents us from yelling instructions at our kids and allows them to make their own choices, to learn through playing the game, and to actually hear their coaches and teammates.

This practice is yet another example of filling emotional tanks and maintaining the magic ratio of five positive interactions to every negative one (chapter 14), both of which are hallmarks of healthy relationships.

I Love to Watch You Play

Here is another supportive-parenting practice. If you google the phrase "I love to watch you play," you will find many well-written articles that will support you in conveying your love for your child and your enjoyment of watching him compete. However, if "I love to watch you play" is the only thing you say after every competition, the phrase will become empty and meaningless. So practice being *specific*: "I loved seeing you…shake off that mistake, hold your own with that tough defender, finish strong, help your opponent up, stick that landing…"

Listen First

In particularly difficult moments, especially when you and your child are in the refractory period (chapter 6), it may be best to simply offer your comforting presence and allow your child to take the lead. This powerful practice is astonishing in its simplicity, and it is often most needed after a particularly devastating performance or loss. Notice when you feel a desperate urge to say something, to make your child feel better, or to comment on her play. Then breathe. Offer your spacious presence. Create the time and space for both you and your child to befriend your feelings (chapter 6). And let your child lead. Nancy Star, writing in the *Washington Post* about raising athletic kids, recognized the power of remaining silent and letting our children lead:

If I see someone is hurting, I'm not shy about acknowledging their pain. What a revelation to discover that's nothing compared to standing as silent witness…

The goal of silence wasn't to prevent conversation. It was to give my daughter space to initiate it. (2017)

Giving Your Child the Gift of Mindfulness

For the next month commit to the following:

- Noticing the physical sensations, thoughts, feelings, and behaviors that indicate you are pressuring rather than supporting

- Acknowledging positives from the past

- Sharing why, specifically, you love to watch your child play

- Listening to your child

- Practicing self-compassion (chapter 9) when you revert to old habits

- Renewing your commitment to being supportive

And for those of you willing to challenge yourself with advanced practice, after you have devoted at least one month to doing the practices with your child you can increase the degree of difficulty by doing the practices with your child's teammates and opponents. Imagine what our children's sports experiences would be like if every parent committed to these practices.

Acknowledgments

I am grateful first and foremost to my beloved coach, Georgina Lindsey, without whom this beautiful offering would not exist; for Jon Kabat-Zinn, Saki Santorelli, and the pioneers at the Stress Reduction Clinic (now the Center for Mindfulness at the University of Massachusetts), for the elegant structure of mindfulness-based stress reduction; for my dear friends and colleagues George Mumford, who brought mindfulness for athletes into the mainstream, and Steve Hickman and Pete Kirchmer, who have given me the opportunity to share mindfulness with athletes and business leaders through mindfulness performance enhancement, awareness, and knowledge (mPEAK) at the Center for Mindfulness, University of California, San Diego; for the wonderful athletes and authors quoted in this book, and those whose quotes didn't make the final cut, who are continuously demonstrating the principles of mindfulness; for my team at New Harbinger Publications, Tesilya Hanauer, Caleb Beckwith, James Lainsbury, Clancy Drake, and Amy Shoup; for my generous and talented illustrator Kristin Wiens; and for you, dear reader, for your commitment to finding flow in sports and in life.

Appendix:
Nine Dots Puzzle Solution

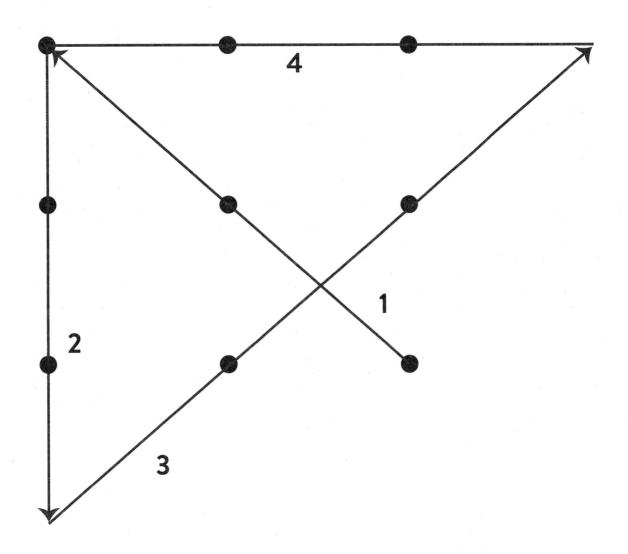

Selected Reading

Afremow, J. 2013. *The Champion's Mind: How Great Athletes Think, Train, and Thrive*. New York: Rodale. In the first half of this book, Afremow offers the skills he uses with elite athletes to enhance their performance. In the second half, he shares compelling stories about various athletes applying these skills in training and competition.

Brown, D. J. 2013. *The Boys in the Boat: Nine Americans and Their Epic Quest for Gold at the 1936 Berlin Olympics*. New York: Penguin Books. This is the intimate and powerful story of nine working-class boys from Washington who overcame the extreme hardships of growing up during the Depression and developed both the grit and the humility to become a true rowing team, ultimately winning the gold medal in the 1936 Olympics.

Chastain, B. 2004. *It's Not About the Bra: Play Hard, Play Fair, and Put the Fun Back into Competitive Sports*. New York: HarperCollins. In this book Chastain humbly shares her experience as an athlete—her challenges, doubts, mistakes, victories, and life lessons and leadership skills she learned as she developed from a youth player into an Olympic gold medalist and World Cup champion.

Gallwey, W. T. 2008. *The Inner Game of Tennis: The Classic Guide to the Mental Side of Peak Performance*. New York: Random House. In this book Gallwey offers detailed suggestions for mastering the inner game—for overcoming self-doubt, nervousness, and lapses of concentration, thereby freeing the body to naturally improve physical performance. Even if tennis isn't your game, the lessons can be applied to any sport.

Green, S. 2011. *The Way of Baseball: Finding Stillness at 95 MPH*. New York: Simon and Schuster. In this book Green describes *how* he developed a mindful swing, which allowed him to set multiple MLB records, and a mindfulness practice, which allowed him to deal with the challenges of "success," "failure," and injury and helped him in his relationships with managers, teammates, fans, and loved ones.

Jackson, P. 2006. *Sacred Hoops: Spiritual Lessons as a Hardwood Warrior*. Rev. ed. New York: Hyperion. In this book Jackson shares the foundations of his philosophy of mindful basketball, offering stories of how he convinced Michael Jordan and the rest of the Bulls to move from "me to we" and go on to win six NBA championships.

Jackson, P. 2014. *Eleven Rings: The Soul of Success*. New York: Penguin Books. In this book Jackson expands on the wisdom he offers in *Sacred Hoops* and shares additional insights from his time coaching both the championship Bulls and Lakers.

Mumford, G. 2015. *The Mindful Athlete: Secrets to Pure Performance*. Berkeley, CA: Parallax Press. In this book Mumford shares his own journey, from playing college basketball, through injury and high-functioning addiction, to teaching mindfulness to prison inmates, and, ultimately, Michael Jordan, Kobe Bryant, the championship Los Angeles Lakers and Chicago Bulls, as well as other elite athletes and corporate executives.

References

Abrams, J. 2015. "Hustle and Flow." Grantland. June 10. http://grantland.com/features /harrison-barnes-nba-finals-2015-golden-state-warriors-cleveland-cavaliers-lebron-james -north-carolina-tar-heels.

Afremow, J. 2013. *The Champion's Mind: How Great Athletes Think, Train, and Thrive.* New York: Rodale.

Agassi, A. 2009. *Open: An Autobiography.* New York: Alfred A. Knopf.

American Academy of Sleep Medicine. 2008. "Ongoing Study Continues to Show That Extra Sleep Improves Athletic Performance." June 9. http://www.aasmnet.org/articles .aspx?id=954.

Baltzell, A. 2016. "Self-Compassion, Distress Tolerance, and Mindfulness in Performance." In *Mindfulness and Performance*, edited by A. L. Baltzell, 53–77. New York: Cambridge University Press.

Bariso, J. 2016. "These 2 NFL Coaches Reacted Very Differently to Their Players' Mistakes—and Taught Us a Major Lesson in Leadership." Inc. October 24. http://www .inc.com/justin-bariso/a-lesson-in-leadership-2-football-coaches-2-player-mistakes-and-2 -very-different.html.

Bastie, F. 2017. "Recruiting Column: Top 5 Things Some Parents Do That Annoy College Coaches." *USA Today*, High School Sports, April 12. http://usatodayhss.com/2017 /recruiting-column-top-5-things-some-parents-do-that-annoy-college-coaches.

Beard, A. 2012. "Bela Karolyi." *Harvard Business Review*, July-August. https://hbr.org/2012 /07/bela-karolyi.

Bernier, M., E. Thienot, R. Codron, and J. F. Fournier. 2009. "Mindfulness and Acceptance Approaches in Sport Performance." *Journal of Clinical Sport Psychology* 4: 320–333.

Block, M. 2016. "After Going for Gold, Athletes Can Feel the Post-Olympic Blues." NPR.org. September 8. http://www.npr.org/sections/thetorch/2016/09/08/493111873/after-going-for -gold-athletes-can-feel-the-post-olympic-blues.

Bonesteel, M. 2015. "The Number of Parents Who Think Their High School Athlete Will Play Pro Sports Is Absurdly High." *Washington Post*, September 9. https://www.washing

tonpost.com/news/early-lead/wp/2015/09/09/the-number-of-parents-who-think-their-high -school-athlete-will-play-pro-sports-is-absurdly-high.

Bowmile, M. 2016. "Santo Condorelli Flips Off His Dad Before Every Race." Swim Swam. January 27. https://swimswam.com/santo-condorelli-flips-off-dad-every-race.

Breines, J. G., and S. Chen. 2012. "Self-Compassion Increases Self-Improvement Motivation." *Personality and Social Psychology Bulletin* 38: 1133–1143.

Brouns, F., W. Saris, and H. Schneider. 1992. "Rationale for Upper Limits of Electrolyte Replacement During Exercise." *International Journal of Sport Nutrition* 2: 229–238.

Brown, D. 2016. "How Stephen Curry's 3-Point Shooting Scores for Kids in Africa." *Mercury News*, April 14. http://www.mercurynews.com/warriors/ci_29768504/how -stephen-currys-3-point-shooting-scores-kids.

Brown, D. J. 2013. *The Boys in the Boat: Nine Americans and Their Epic Quest for Gold at the 1936 Berlin Olympics.* New York: Penguin Books.

Brown, E. No date. "How Much Sugar Should Your Sports Drink Contain? Research on Carbohydrate Concentration, Sugar Combination and Impact on Marathon Performance." Runners Connect. Accessed May 1, 2017. http://runnersconnect.net /running-nutrition-articles/best-sports-drink-marathon.

Buzinski, J. 2013. "Rating the Best and Worst Apologies of Athletes Who Made Gay Slurs." Outsports. June 6. http://www.outsports.com/2013/6/6/4397988/athlete-gay-slurs-best -worst-apologies-kobe-roy-hibbert-roddy-white.

Carlisle, J. 2015. "How Getting Cut Helped Carli Lloyd Refocus and Find Her Spot on the USWNT." ESPNW. June 3. http://www.espn.com/espnw/news-commentary/ 2015worldcup/article/13006977/how-getting-cut-helped-carli-lloyd-refocus-find -spot-us-women-national-team.

Carmichael, S. G. 2015. "How to Coach, According to 5 Great Sports Coaches." *Harvard Business Review*, February 25. https://hbr.org/2015/02/how-to-coach-according -to-5-great-sports-coaches.

Chastain, B. 2004. *It's Not About the Bra: Play Hard, Play Fair, and Put the Fun Back into Competitive Sports.* New York: HarperCollins.

Chastain, B. 2015. "Letter to My Younger Self." Players' Tribune. July 7. http://www.the playerstribune.com/brandi-chastain-letter-to-my-younger-self.

Chödrön, P. 2002. *Comfortable with Uncertainty: 108 Teachings on Fearlessness and Compassion.* Boston: Shambala Publications.

Csikzszentmihalyi, M. 2009. *Flow: The Psychology of Optimal Experience.* New York. Harper and Row.

Dampf, A. No date. "Vonn Apologizes After Destroying Ski with Hammer in Video." *Sports Illustrated.* https://www.si.com/2016/02/20/ap-ski-vonn-apology.

Ekman, P. 2007. *Emotions Revealed: Recognizing Faces and Feelings to Improve Communication and Emotional Life.* 2nd ed. New York: Henry Holt.

Fatigue Science. 2015. "Jet Lag's Impact on Athlete Performance: Part 3." *Fatigue Science* (blog). December 10. http://www.fatiguescience.com/blog/jet-lags-impact-on-athletic-performance-part-3.

Ferguson, L. J., K. C. Kowalski, D. E. Mack, and C. M. Sabiston. 2014. "Exploring Self-Compassion and Eudaimonic Well-Being in Young Women Athletes." *Journal of Sport and Exercise Psychology* 36: 203–216.

Florio, J., and O. Shapiro. 2016. "The Dark Side of Going for the Gold." *Atlantic,* August 18. http://www.theatlantic.com/health/archive/2016/08/post-olympic-depression/496244.

Frank, N. 2016. "Steve Kerr, Luke Walton and the Positive Coaching Legacy Leading the Warriors." WTOP. February 29. http://wtop.com/nba/2016/02/steve-kerr-luke-walton-and-the-positive-coaching-legacy-leading-the-warriors.

Frye, C. 2017. "Sorry for Yelling, Now Let's Go Get a Juice Box." Players' Tribune. April 14. https://www.theplayerstribune.com/channing-frye-cavaliers-playoffs.

Gallagher, T. 2016. "Wrestler Accepts Forfeit in Honor of Late Spencer Foe." *Sioux City Journal,* January 12. http://m.siouxcityjournal.com/news/local/columnists/gallagher/gallagher-wrestler-accepts-forfeit-in-honor-of-late-spencer-foe/article_995d295f-8554-598a-8e1b-d8e292628133.html?utm_source=twitterfeed&utm_medium=facebook&mobile_touch=true.

Gallwey, W. T. 2008. *The Inner Game of Tennis: The Classic Guide to the Mental Side of Peak Performance.* New York: Random House.

Gibbs, L. 2016. "Serena Williams' Inspiring Defeat." Think Progress. January 30. http://thinkprogress.org/sports/2016/01/30/3744575/serena-williams-sportsmanship.

Gooding, A., and F. L. Gardner. 2009. "An Investigation of the Relationship Between Mindfulness, Preshot Routine, and Basketball Free Throw Percentage." *Journal of Clinical Sport Psychology* 3: 303–319.

Gottman, J. M. 1994. *What Predicts Divorce: The Relationship Between Marital Processes and Marital Outcomes.* New York: Lawrence Erlbaum.

Green, S. 2011. *The Way of Baseball: Finding Stillness at 95 MPH.* New York: Simon and Schuster.

Haase, L., A. C. May, M. Falahpour, S. Isakovic, A. N. Simmons, S. D. Hickman, T. T. Liu, and M. P. Paulus. 2015. "A Pilot Study Investigating Changes in Neural Processing After Mindfulness Training in Elite Athletes." *Frontiers in Behavioral Neuroscience* 9: Article 229.

Heffernan, L., and J. B. Wallace. 2016. "What College Sports Recruiters Can Teach Your Child." *New York Times, Well* (blog). June 21. https://well.blogs.nytimes.com/2016/06/21/what-college-sports-recruiters-can-teach-your-child.

Holmes, B. 2015. "Kobe Talks Evolution of Empathy, Understanding for Teammates." ESPN. December 27. http://espn.go.com/nba/story/_/id/14448863/kobe-bryant-los-angeles-lakers-says-advise-rookie-self-understand-compassion-empathy.

Hubbling, A., M. Reilly-Spong, M. J. Kreitzer, and C. R. Gross. 2014. "How Mindfulness Changed My Sleep: Focus Groups with Chronic Insomnia Patients." *BMC Complementary and Alternative Medicine* 14: 50.

Ivarsson, A., U. Johnson, M. B. Andersen, J. Fallby, and M. Altemyr. 2015. "It Pays to Pay Attention: A Mindfulness-Based Program for Injury Prevention with Soccer Players." *Journal of Applied Sport Psychology* 27: 319–334.

Jackson, P. 2014. *Eleven Rings: The Soul of Success*. New York: Penguin Books.

Jackson, S. 2016. "Flow and Mindfulness in Performance." In *Mindfulness and Performance*, edited by A. L. Baltzell, 78–100. New York: Cambridge University Press.

Jeukendrup, A., and M. Gleeson. 2010. *Sport Nutrition: An Introduction to Energy Production and Performance*. 2nd ed. Champaign, IL: Human Kinetics.

John, S., S. K. Verma, and G. L. Khanna. 2011. "The Effect of Mindfulness Meditation on HPA-Axis in Pre-Competition Stress in Sports Performance of Elite Shooters." *National Journal of Integrated Research in Medicine* 2: 15–21.

Kabat-Zinn, J., B. Beall, and J. Rippe. 1985. "A Systematic Mental Training Program Based on Mindfulness Meditation, to Optimize Performance in Collegiate and Olympic Rowers." Poster session presented at the World Congress in Sport Psychology, Copenhagen, Denmark, June.

Kanters, M. A., J. Bocarro, and J. M. Casper. 2008. "Supported or Pressured? An Examination of Agreement Among Parents and Children on Parent's Role in Youth Sports." *Journal of Sport Behavior* 31: 64–80.

Kaufman, K., C. R. Glass, and T. R. Pineau. 2016. "Mindful Sport Performance Enhancement (MSPE)." In *Mindfulness and Performance*, edited by A. L. Baltzell, 153–185. New York: Cambridge University Press.

Kawakami, T. 2015. "Luke Walton, Steve Kerr and the Warriors' Four Core Values: Joy, Mindfulness, Compassion and Competition." *Mercury News, Talking Points* (blog). November 24. http://blogs.mercurynews.com/kawakami/2015/11/24/luke-walton-steve-kerr-and-the-warriors-four-core-values-joy-mindfulness-compassion-and-competition.

Kerr-Dineen, L. 2015. "Jordan Spieth Gave the Most Humble Response Ever After Winning $10 Million." *USA Today Sports*, For the Win, September 28. http://ftw.usatoday.com /2015/09/jordan-spieth-gave-the-most-humble-response-ever-after-winning-10-million.

Kiefer, D. No date. "The Artist." Gostanford.com. http://www.gostanford.com/index.aspx.

Knight, C. J., C. M. Boden, and N. L. Holt. 2010. "Junior Tennis Players' Preferences for Parental Behaviors." *Journal of Applied Sports Psychology* 22. DOI: 10.1080/10413200 .2010.495324.

Leung, D. 2015. "Tech Wins a Starting Spot for Warriors." *Mercury News*, November 17. http://www.pressreader.com/usa/the-mercury-news/20151117/281479275312525.

Lichtman, C. 2016. "Chapters." *Musings of a Vagabond* (blog). July 1. http://cassidylichtman .blogspot.com/2016/07/chapters.html.

Litman, L. 2015. "How Julie Johnston's Worst Nightmare Sparked a Victory Over Germany." *USA Today*, July 1. http://ftw.usatoday.com/2015/07/how-julie-johnstons-worst-nightmare -sparked-a-victory-over-germany.

Lloyd, C., and W. Coffey. 2016. *When Nobody Was Watching: My Hard-Fought Journey to the Top of the Soccer World*. New York: Houghton Mifflin Harcourt.

Losada, M. 1999. "The Complex Dynamics of High Performance Teams." *Mathematical and Computer Modelling* 30: 179–192.

Losada, M., and E. Heaphy. 2004. "The Role of Positivity and Connectivity in the Performance of Business Teams: A Nonlinear Dynamics Model." *American Behavioral Scientist* 47: 740–765.

Mah, C. D., K. E. Mah, E. J. Kezirian, and W. C. Dement. 2011. "The Effects of Sleep Extension on the Athletic Performance of Collegiate Basketball Players." *Sleep* 34: 943–950.

Mape, A. 2016. "My Parents Made Me into a Professional Athlete." I Love to Watch You Play. April 5. http://ilovetowatchyouplay.com/2016/04/05/my-parents-made-me-into -a-professional-athlete.

Mazeika, V. 2015. "Stanford Football: Owusu's Catch Defies Logic, Not Science." *Mercury News*, October 21. http://www.mercurynews.com/2015/10/21/stanford-football -owusus-catch-defies-logic-not-science.

McArdle, W. D., F. I. Katch, and V. L. Katch. 2007. *Exercise Physiology, Energy, Nutrition, and Human Performance*. 6th ed. Baltimore: Lippincott, Williams, and Wilkins.

Moore, Z. E. 2016. "Mindfulness, Emotion Regulation, and Performance." In *Mindfulness and Performance*, edited by A. L. Baltzell, 29–52. New York: Cambridge University Press.

Mosewich, A. D., P. R. E. Crocker, K. C. Kowalski, and A. DeLongis. 2013. "Applying Self-Compassion in Sport: An Intervention with Women Athletes." *Journal of Sport and Exercise Psychology* 35: 514–524.

Mosewich, A. D., K. C. Kowalski, C. M. Sabiston, W. A. Sedgwick, and J. L. Tracy. 2011. "Self-Compassion: A Potential Resource for Young Women Athletes." *Journal of Sport and Exercise Psychology* 33: 103–123.

Mumford G. 2015. *The Mindful Athlete: Secrets to Pure Performance.* Berkeley, CA: Parallax Press.

NCAA. 2017. "Estimated Probability of Competing in College Athletics." NCAA. March 10. http://www.ncaa.org/about/resources/research/estimated-probability-competing -college-athletics.

Neff, K. D. 2011. *Self-Compassion: The Proven Power of Being Kind to Yourself.* New York: HarperCollins.

Neff, K. D., Y.-P. Hsieh, and K. Dejitterat. 2005. "Self-Compassion, Achievement Goals, and Coping with Academic Failure." *Self and Identity* 4: 263–287.

NPR. 2016. "Remembering the 'Great Santini' Author Pat Conroy." *Fresh Air.* March 11. http://www.npr.org/2016/03/11/469944762/remembering-great-santini-author-pat-conroy.

NPR, Robert Wood Johnson Foundation, and Harvard T. H. Chan School of Public Health, eds. 2015. "Sports and Health in America." Public opinion poll series. http://www.rwjf .org/en/library/research/2015/06/sports-and-health-in-america.html.

Orr, C. 2016. "Tony Romo: Dak Prescott's Earned Right to Be QB." NFL.com. November 15. http://www.nfl.com/news/story/0ap3000000740373/article/tony-romo-dak-prescotts -earned-right-to-be-qb.

O'Sullivan, J. 2015. "The One Quality Great Teammates Have in Common." Changing the Game Project. October 13. http://changingthegameproject.com/the-one-quality -great-teammates-have-in-common.

Park, A. 2016. "The Olympic Gymnast Who Overcame a Drug-Addicted Mother." *Time,* June 2. http://time.com/collection-post/4352599/simone-biles-next-generation-leaders.

Peterson, G. 2016. "Warriors' Draymond Green Schools Oakland High Students." *Mercury News,* October 12. http://www.mercurynews.com/2016/10/12/warriors -draymond-green-schools-oakland-high-students.

Proactive Coaching. 2015. "Good teams don't have an 'in group' and an 'out group.'" Facebook post. October 26. Accessed May 1, 2017. https://www.facebook.com/proactive coach.

Reis, N. A., K. C. Kowalski, L. J. Ferguson, C. M. Sabiston, W. A. Sedgwick, and P. R. E. Crocker. 2015. "Self-Compassion and Women Athletes' Responses to Emotionally Difficult Sport Situations: An Evaluation of Brief Induction." *Psychology of Sport and Exercise* 16: 18–25.

Riley, L., and L. Dillman. 2014. "Lindsey Jacobellis Back for More in Snowboard Cross at Sochi Olympics." *Los Angeles Times*, February 15. http://articles.latimes.com/2014/feb/15 /news/la-lindsey-jacobellis-back-for-more-in-snowboard-cross-at-sochi-olympics-20140215.

Samuels, D. 2016. "7 Things That College Coaches Want to See in a Prospect's Social Media." Footballscoop.com. June 27. http://footballscoop.com/news/7-things-college -coaches-want-see-high-school-recruits-social-media.

Scott, N. 2016. "Jack Sock Gives Point to Lleyton Hewitt in Incredible Moment of Sportsmanship." *USA Today*, January 6. http://ftw.usatoday.com/2016/01/jack-sock-gives-point -to-lleyton-hewitt-in-incredible-moment-of-sportsmanship.

Scott-Hamilton, J., N. S. Schutte, and R. F. Brown. 2016. "Effects of a Mindfulness Intervention on Sports-Anxiety, Pessimism, and Flow in Competitive Cyclists." *Applied Psychology: Health and Well-Being* 8: 85–103.

Shipnuck, A. 2016. "Stephen Curry and Wife Ayesha on Marriage, Kids and Their Matching Tattoos." *Parents Magazine*. http://www.parents.com/parenting/celebrity-parents/moms -dads/stephen-curry-wife-ayesha-on-marriage-kids-matching-tattoos.

Star, N. 2017. "The First Rule of Sports (and All) Parenting: Don't Speak." *Washington Post*, February 28. https://www.washingtonpost.com/news/parenting/wp/2017/02/28/the-first -rule-of-sports-and-all-parenting-dont-speak/?utm_term=.eafb29b627b0.

Stepp, J. 2016. "Came across an awful Twitter account today. Shame the kid was a really good player … On to the next … get a clue." Coachjstepp. January 8. 8:09 a.m. Tweet. https://twitter.com/coachjstepp/status/685493484967477248.

Stickells, L. 2015. "Greater Than Gold: Elizabeth Price Realizes Life Beyond the Olympics." *Stanford Daily*, January 29. http://www.stanforddaily.com/greater-than-gold-elizabeth -price-realizes-life-beyond-the-olympics.

Summitt, P., and S. Jenkins. 1998. *Reach for the Summit: The Definite Dozen System for Succeeding at Whatever You Do.* New York: Broadway Books.

Talansky, A. 2016. "I'm Back!" *Andrew Talansky* (blog). October 19. http://www.andrew -talansky.com/blog/2016/10/19/back.

Taylor, J. 2012. "Sport Imagery: Athletes' Most Powerful Mental Tool." *Psychology Today*, November 6. https://www.psychologytoday.com/blog/the-power-prime/201211/sport -imagery-athletes-most-powerful-mental-tool.

Thompson, J. 2011. *Elevating Your Game: Becoming a Triple-Impact Competitor.* Portola Valley, CA: Balance Sports Publishing.

Thompson, M. 2015. "Stephen Curry's Long, Long Road to NBA MVP." *Mercury News,* May 4. http://blogs.mercurynews.com/thompson/2015/05/04/stephen-currys-long-long-road-nba-mvp.

Time Staff. 2017. "Theo Epstein at Yale Class Day: 'Choose to Keep Your Heads Up.'" *Time,* May 22. http://time.com/4787640/theo-epstein-cubs-yale-graduation-commencement.

Van Bibber, R. 2014. "The Worst of the Richie Incognito/Jonathan Martin Report." SB Nation. February 14. http://www.sbnation.com/nfl/2014/2/14/5411608/worst-of-the-richie-incognito-jonathan-martin-report-miami-dolphins.

Ward-Henninger, C. 2016. "Rio Olympics 2016: Michael Phelps Wins Gold in Final Race of Career." CBSSports. August 14. https://www.cbssports.com/olympics/news/rio-olympics-2016-michael-phelps-wins-gold-in-final-race-of-career.

Wilner, J. 2015. "Shaw Starting to Shed His Dispassionate Demeanor." *Mercury News,* October 24. http://www.pressreader.com/usa/the-mercury-news/20151024/282097750561207.

Women's Health. 2012. "Olympians Share Their Personal Mantras: Find Out What Motivates These Winning Women." *Women's Health,* June 29. http://www.womenshealthmag.com/fitness/motivational-quotes-0

Wooden, J., and J. Reger. 2002. *Quotable Wooden: Words of Wisdom, Preparation, and Success by and About John Wooden, College Basketball's Greatest Coach.* Lanham, MD: Taylor Trade.

Wyshynski, G. 2016. "Kerri Walsh Jennings, the Anti–Hope Solo in First Olympic Defeat." Yahoo! Sports. August 16. http://sports.yahoo.com/news/kerri-walsh-jennings-the-anti-hope-solo-in-1st-olympic-defeat-055546879.html.

Yesu, L., and E. A. Harwood. 2015. "The Effects of Parental Involvement, Support, and Pressure on Athletic Participation." *InSight: Rivier Academic Journal* 11: 1–12. agassihttp://www.rivier.edu/Journal/ROAJ-Spring-2015/J914_Yesu_Harwood.pdf.

Yoon, J. S., E. Barton, and J. Taiariol. 2004. "Relational Aggression in Middle School: Educational Implications of Developmental Research." *Journal of Early Adolescence* 24: 303–318.

Young, S. 2011. *Natural Pain Relief: How to Soothe and Dissolve Physical Pain with Mindfulness.* Boulder, CO: Sounds True.

Amy Saltzman, MD, is a longtime athlete, holistic physician, mindfulness coach, wife, mother, devoted student of transformation, and occasional poet. Starting in junior high, Saltzman participated in and coached gymnastics; in college, she earned a spot as a walk-on varsity gymnast at Stanford University. Later she turned to competitive cycling, and has been a recreational athlete (cycling, running, yoga, and snowboarding) for years. She is the mother of one professional athlete and one performing artist.

She is recognized as a visionary and pioneer in the field of mindfulness for youth. She is founder and director of the Association for Mindfulness in Education; an inaugural and longstanding member of the steering committee for the Mindfulness in Education Network; and founding member of the Northern California Advisory Committee on Mindfulness.

As a mindfulness coach, Saltzman's passion is supporting people of all ages in finding flow. She resides in the San Francisco Bay Area, where she provides holistic medical care and mindfulness coaching. She is available in person and via the web to offer introductory presentations, workshops, and eight-week courses to individuals and teams aspiring to enhance their performance in any domain. For more information, visit www.stillquietplace.com.

Foreword writer **Jim Thompson** is founder and CEO of Positive Coaching Alliance (PCA). PCA's vision of youth sports as a Development Zone has attracted the support and involvement of many elite coaches, athletes, academics, and business leaders in this country. Thompson received the inaugural ETHOS Award from the Institute for Sports Law and Ethics (ISLE) in 2013. He also serves on the faculty of Stanford University's continuing studies program, where he teaches courses in coaching, leadership, and sport and spirituality.

MORE BOOKS *from*
NEW HARBINGER PUBLICATIONS

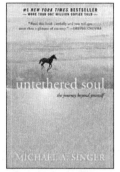

Register your **new harbinger** titles for additional benefits!

When you register your **new harbinger** title—purchased in any format, from any source—you get access to benefits like the following:

- Downloadable accessories like printable worksheets and extra content

- Instructional videos and audio files

- Information about updates, corrections, and new editions

Not every title has accessories, but we're adding new material all the time.

Access free accessories in 3 easy steps:

1. Sign in at NewHarbinger.com (or **register** to create an account).

2. Click on **register a book**. Search for your title and click the **register** button when it appears.

3. Click on the **book cover or title** to go to its details page. Click on **accessories** to view and access files.

That's all there is to it!

If you need help, visit:

NewHarbinger.com/accessories

new harbinger
CELEBRATING
40 YEARS